Dance We Must

Dance We Must

The Art and Costumes of Ruth St. Denis and Ted Shawn, 1906–1940

EDITED BY
Kevin M. Murphy and
Caroline Hamilton

WITH ADDITIONAL CONTRIBUTIONS BY
Erica Dankmeyer
Panalee Maskati
Norton Owen
Thandi Steele
Munjulika R. Tarah

WILLIAMS COLLEGE MUSEUM OF ART
WILLIAMSTOWN, MASSACHUSETTS

Contents

Director's Foreword & Acknowledgements

In 2018, the Williams College Museum of Art (WCMA) and Jacob's Pillow collaborated on the exhibition *Dance We Must: Treasures from Jacob's Pillow, 1906–1940*, which focused on the material culture created by and for Jacob's Pillow founder Ted Shawn and pioneering modern dancer Ruth St. Denis. Shawn and St. Denis were partners in life and dance from 1914 to 1931 and together founded Denishawn, the first significant dance company in the United States. After the end of the couple's personal and professional relationship, Shawn went on to form his Men Dancers company, centered at a farmhouse that Shawn had purchased in Becket, Massachusetts, in southern Berkshire County. In the Berkshire hills, Shawn also started the Jacob's Pillow Dance Festival, which remains a leading venue for all forms of dance today. The materials in *Dance We Must*, curated by Kevin M. Murphy, Eugénie Prendergast Senior Curator of American and European Art at WCMA, and Caroline Hamilton, a dance historian specializing in costume who is costume curator at Jacob's Pillow, were drawn almost entirely from the Jacob's Pillow Dance Festival Archives. The exhibition marked the first time that the full wealth of the collections—including art, photography, costumes, props, sets, promotional materials, and ephemera—had been on view. Many of these objects, in particular the costumes, had not been examined for decades and were being fully catalogued for the first time.

The project was a natural fit for WCMA, which has a core mission of teaching with and interpreting objects from interdisciplinary perspectives, and for Williams College, which has a long history of strong academic and performance programs in dance and theater. The materials from Jacob's Pillow provided a rich opportunity to contribute to the scholarship of early modern dance in the United States while engaging students, faculty, and community audiences alike. The exhibition also brought together the two major strengths of cultural institutions in the Berkshires: performance and the visual arts.

As the exhibition curators worked on the checklist, it became apparent that the materials they were finding surfaced legacies of colonialism, cultural appropriation, and racism in dance, art, and American history. Students, faculty, and staff in 2018 discussed St. Denis, Shawn, and the role of institutions like WCMA, Williams, and Jacob's Pillow in promoting—consciously or not—racist and Orientalist ideologies. These difficult conversations feel even more urgent now. The Jacob's Pillow Archives are a critical resource for studying the troubled—and troubling—histories of dance, art, and culture in the early twentieth-century United States and beyond. Murphy and Hamilton realized that the short span and limited interpretive tools of an exhibition were inadequate in conveying the importance of the materials in the archives, yet the sheer volume and variety of materials they pulled from old touring trunks and scrapbooks precluded a publication in 2018. This 2022 book expands on the themes of the exhibition, presents new research, and includes the perspectives of Williams faculty and students who taught with, danced alongside, and, at times, critiqued aspects of the materials' presentation at WCMA.

In the book's first section, Norton Owen, director of preservation at Jacob's Pillow, provides an account of Shawn's self-conscious desire to safeguard his legacy. Alongside correspondence and business records retained by Shawn and materials preserved by happenstance, Owen's own contributions in building the collections over decades have made Jacob's Pillow's holdings a rich and unique archive of dance in the United States.

Next, Caroline Hamilton introduces the importance of costume to St. Denis and Shawn. They employed a mixture of improvisation and ingenuity along with the voracious acquisition of textiles and jewelry from around the world to create the outfits they wore on stage. In many of their dances, costumes were as important as choreography and, in some cases, helped dictate how the dancers could move. Hamilton also wrote short essays that are interspersed throughout the book and detail the construction and origin of a selection of costumes plus a makeup box belonging to a Denishawn dancer.

Murphy traces St. Denis's and Shawn's collaboration with painters, sculptors, printmakers, and photographers, from St. Denis's early solo career, when she modeled for artists such as Auguste Rodin, through the end of Shawn's Men Dancers in 1940. The essay demonstrates how the dancers relied on artists to help shape their public images, while artists often found new modes of expression through their depictions of the dancers.

Finally, Assistant Professor of Dance Munjulika Tarah and Artist-in-Residence in Dance Erica Dankmeyer, in dialogue with Williams students Thandi Steele '22 and Panalee Maskati '20, discuss how they included the exhibition in their teaching of the history and practice of dance. Dankmeyer and Maskati performed St. Denis solos at the exhibition opening and speak to the experience of dancing this Orientalist work in the twenty-first century from their intersectional positions. The discussion highlights the tensions and contradictions between the often-beautiful materials on display in 2018 and St. Denis's and Shawn's misrepresentation of Asian, African, and Indigenous American cultures.

This publication represents the heart of WCMA's mission to generate new scholarship, to explore across disciplines, and to collaborate with our exceptional partners in the vibrant, arts-rich region we call home. It also speaks to our desire and commitment to ask critical questions, to challenge assumptions, and to respect the complexities of personal, institutional, and societal histories while not allowing injustices or falsehoods to have any place or influence in our contemporary understandings.

Installation view of the *Dance We Must* exhibition, Williams College Museum of Art, 2018.

From those who worked to create the exhibition in 2018 to the cross-institutional collaborators on this volume, a legion of people have helped realize this project. While our gratitude extends to the entire staffs of both WCMA and the Jacob's Pillow Dance Festival, we would like to single out the following individuals for their contributions: at WCMA, Nathan Ahern, Sara Bonthius, Lisa Dorin, Alex Groff, Diane Hart, Will Hernandez MA '19, Emma Jacobs MA '20, Emily Kamen MA '20, Adi Nachman, Christina Olson, Nina Pelaez, Eve Rosekind MA '19, Elizabeth Sandoval, and Jessie Sentivan; and at Jacob's Pillow, Patsy Gay, Norton Owen, Pamela Tatge, and Nicole Tomasofsky. We are grateful to Williams College faculty members Sandra L. Burton, David Gürçay-Morris, and Janine Parker; and to Maggie Barkovic, Mary Catherine Betz, and Hugh Glover at the Williamstown Art Conservation Center. We are also indebted to the lenders to the exhibition in 2018, including Chapin Library and Special Collections, Williams College; the Hon. Stephen P. Driscoll; Patsy Gay; the National Museum of Dance, Saratoga Springs, New York; and Norton Owen. Joan and Jim Hunter have our continued appreciation for providing crucial support for the exhibition, in honor of Norton Owen.

I am deeply grateful to the Coby Foundation, Ltd. for their support of this publication, enabling a more fulsome consideration of the exhibition material and a significant contribution to the literature in the history of American dance and visual arts. Its production benefitted from the expertise of editor Kristin Swan and the staff of Lucia | Marquand: Leah Finger, Melissa Duffes, Adrian Lucia, Ryan Polich, and Kestrel Rundle. I thank Kevin Murphy for leading this project—from his passionate advocacy for the book at the outset, to gathering contributions from such a talented ensemble of scholars, both emerging and seasoned, to ensuring that a range of perspectives are brought to bear on the vital issues at play in this volume.

And, finally, I wish to thank our dear friends and partners at Jacob's Pillow once more for the *Dance We Must* collaboration in all its forms: exhibition, programs, and now publication. I am thrilled by the possibilities that the future holds for bringing the treasures of our respective organizations—the collections, the people, and the programs—together again in similarly creative and generative ways.

Pamela Franks
Class of 1956 Director
Williams College Museum of Art

Introduction

The Story of the Jacob's Pillow Dance Festival Archives

Norton Owen

Although many ideas of Jacob's Pillow founder Ted Shawn (1891–1972; fig. 1.1) were revolutionary in their time, and Shawn is credited with a number of important "firsts" during his career, he was also a devoted student of history. For nearly four decades after the Pillow opened to the public in 1933, Shawn prefaced each performance with a talk to provide the audience with some historical perspective for what they were about to witness. He had been a theological student before becoming a dancer, and he brought an evangelical zeal to the task of introducing people to dance as an art form that deserved the same respect as music or drama.

That dance had value as anything other than a frivolous pastime was hardly a foregone conclusion in the early part of the twentieth century, and Shawn set out to change that by allying himself with Ruth St. Denis (1879–1968) and establishing Denishawn as the first professional concert dance company in the United States. Both Shawn and St. Denis looked to other cultures as a way of positioning dance within a global context and demonstrating the universality of their chosen vocation. After touring with St. Denis to hundreds of cities throughout the United States and training a subsequent generation of dance innovators including Martha Graham (1894–1991; fig. 1.2), Doris Humphrey (1895–1958), Jack Cole (1911–1974), and others, Shawn moved on to another challenge, setting out to affirm dance as a legitimate career choice for men. His new company, known as Ted Shawn and His Men Dancers, performed as extensively as Denishawn had, on the stages of renowned concert halls and Broadway theaters as well as in high school auditoriums and town halls, returning each summer to its training camp at Jacob's Pillow in Becket, Massachusetts (fig. 1.3).

These formative chapters in American dance history are inextricably woven into the DNA of today's Jacob's Pillow, a thriving international dance festival and school still inhabiting some of the same buildings that the Men Dancers built or adapted in the 1930s. There is little chance for contemporary Pillow visitors to miss the fact that history is all around, from the eighteenth-century farm buildings that populate the site to the old posters and photographs that line the walls of each structure. Past and present coexist at every turn, subtly but unmistakably reminding us that dance has been happening on this site since the field of American concert dance was in its infancy.

This history was examined and celebrated in the remarkable *Dance We Must* exhibition at the Williams College Museum of Art (WCMA) and memorialized in the photographs and text contained in this volume. Visitors to that exhibition were astounded to see costumes, sets, and artifacts from the Jacob's Pillow Dance Festival Archives that few realized had been preserved. For many, seeing these garments and other tangible evidence of the beginnings of American dance was a purely joyful discovery, while some were troubled by outdated depictions of other cultures.

In order to better appreciate the contents of the exhibition, it is important to briefly trace the history of the Pillow Archives and how its countless artifacts came to be saved. I first attempted to tell this story in a 1996 essay, published by the Theatre Library Association, titled "Accidental Acquisitions: The Jacob's Pillow Archive Collection."[1] The first part of the title is key, as much about the history of the Pillow Archives was indeed happenstance. But while the current archives might have evolved haphazardly, the building blocks were always at hand, beginning with Ted Shawn's predisposition toward documentation—an interest that may first have been stoked by his employment, as a teenager, at the Denver Public Library. Shawn had the foresight to preserve some of his dances on film as early as 1913. After he met Ruth St. Denis the following year, Shawn took it upon himself to organize the photographs and programs that she had carelessly stashed in a closet, and he would later lovingly compile and publish a lavish two-volume summary of her career titled *Ruth St. Denis: Pioneer and Prophet*.

This deep-seated urge to capture and memorialize his artistic output permeated the Denishawn years (1915–31) and continued through the Men Dancers era of the 1930s. A flyer from 1938, headlined "Friends have repeatedly asked us if we have recorded our dances on moving picture film," makes a pitch for contributions to help fund this effort. One paragraph reads: "There is much talk these days of a Museum of the Dance, and of the founding of a library of films of great dancers. If and when such an organization is formed, a complete record of the dances of Shawn and His Men Dancers would be a valuable contribution to the literature of the dance."[2] The Men Dancers repertory was indeed recorded on silent film; another fifty years would pass before the company's composer-accompanist, Jess Meeker (1911–1997), created soundtracks for the recordings. While this filmmaking was intentional, many other components of the Pillow Archives were more incidental. Shawn saved all his incoming correspondence and many carbon copies of his own letters, methodically placing all these papers into cardboard boxes marked "Answered Mail" by year. Likewise, he kept thousands of 8 × 10 press photographs long after the need for publicizing a particular engagement had ended. Thus, the Pillow's voluminous holdings of documents and photographs began to accumulate.

There is no evidence that Shawn, during his lifetime, ever considered establishing an onsite archive along the lines of what exists today at Jacob's Pillow. Instead, he nurtured an ongoing relationship with the New York Public Library's Dance Collection, now known as the Jerome Robbins Dance Division, a connection that began in 1950 with the library's founding dance curator, Genevieve Oswald. Shawn's contributions to the library were so extensive and valuable that his name was inscribed on a column in the main branch's

FIG. 1.1
Nickolas Muray (American, born Hungary, 1892–1965), *Ted Shawn in the Dervish Solo from The Vision of the Aissoua*, c. 1924, photograph, 13 × 10¼ in. (33 × 26 cm). Jacob's Pillow Dance Festival Archives.

FIG. 1.2, FACING
Arthur F. Kales (American, 1882–1936), *Ted Shawn and Martha Graham in Malagueña*, c. 1921, photograph, 10 × 8 in. (25.4 × 20.3 cm). Jacob's Pillow Dance Festival Archives.

FIG. 1.3
Richard Merrill (American, 20th century), *Ted Shawn Instructing the Men Dancers at Jacob's Pillow*, 1936, photograph, 10¼ × 13⅝ in. (26 × 34.6 cm). Jacob's Pillow Dance Festival Archives.

Founder's Hall, and yet much material still remained at the Pillow and at Shawn's winter home in Florida.

As for the many trunks full of costumes from Denishawn and the Men Dancers now in the archives (figs. 1.4, 2.1), the reasons for keeping these were purely utilitarian, with the idea of repurposing them at some undefinable future date. Caroline Hamilton writes more extensively about the origins and developments of these costume collections elsewhere in this volume, but it seems important here to point out the commonality between the various types of materials that form the nucleus of the Pillow Archives. The institutional attitude toward all these holdings was more or less one of benign neglect for many years. It would have required more effort to dispose of everything than was necessary simply to leave it where it was. As a result, all of it remained in various unheated sheds and storage areas for more than two decades after Shawn's death.

During the 1980s, I was involved in various efforts to deal with all the accumulated materials, including a National Endowment for the Humanities project to survey the collection, establishing an Archives Committee of the Board, and conducting serious discussions with Genevieve Oswald about transferring all of the Pillow's archival assets to the New York Public Library. After I was appointed as the part-time director of preservation in 1990, a major turning point came with the donation of Blake's Barn, a nineteenth-century structure that was moved to the Pillow site, with exhibition space that could focus attention on the Pillow's holdings. In 1996, unused rooms in Blake's Barn were cobbled together to serve as the first public space for the archives.

FIG. 1.4
Men Dancers original touring trunk detail, with baggage label. Jacob's Pillow Dance Festival Archives.

FIG. 1.5
John Lindquist (American, 1890–1980), *Pre-performance Social Hour at Jacob's Pillow*, c. 1946, photograph, 8 × 9⅞ in. (20.3 × 25.1 cm). Jacob's Pillow Dance Festival Archives.

The visibility of and interest in the Pillow Archives have grown steadily ever since, both onsite and online, and it now seems inconceivable that these resources were not always readily available. Visitors can access the Pillow's past just as easily as they can witness its present, and this characteristic blending of eras makes it possible for even first-time dance-goers to experience the art form as part of a seamless continuum.

The WCMA exhibition's title, *Dance We Must*, was derived directly from Ted Shawn, who published a series of lectures under the same title in 1940. In that volume's opening chapter, "Why Do We Dance?," Shawn declares, "As long as there is life there is movement, and to move is hence to satisfy a basic and eternal need."[3] Shawn's founding vision still informs the Pillow's activities to this day (fig. 1.5), and the adoption of his words to describe this exhibition and its catalogue is an acknowledgement that his passion for dance remains palpable more than a half century after his death.

Notes

1. Norton Owen, "Accidental Acquisitions: The Jacob's Pillow Archive Collection," in *After the Dance: Documents of Ruth St. Denis and Ted Shawn*, Performing Arts Resources, vol. 20, ed. Susan Brady (New York: Theatre Library Association, 1996), 39–56.

2. Program Files, 1938, Jacob's Pillow Dance Festival Archives.

3. Ted Shawn, *Dance We Must* (1940; repr., New York: Haskell House, 1940), 3.

The Legend of the Peacock, 1914

CHOREOGRAPHER
Ruth St. Denis

COMPOSER
Edmund Roth

Bodice and skirt worn by Ruth St. Denis in *The Legend of the Peacock*, 1914–40s; replica headdress created by Quinn Czejkowski, 2018

Cotton brocade, lamé, silk, gelatin and plastic sequins, ceramic and plastic beads, metal, glass

Ruth St. Denis UCLA Costume Collection, Jacob's Pillow Dance Festival Archives, C-001_a-j

ABOVE
Front view of bodice, skirt, and replica headdress, C-000_a-b.

FACING
Robert Henri (American, 1865–1925), *Ruth St. Denis in the Peacock Dance*, 1919, oil on canvas, 85 × 49 in. (215.9 × 124.46 cm). Pennsylvania Academy of the Fine Arts; Gift of the Sameric Corporation in memory of Eric Shapiro, 1976.1.

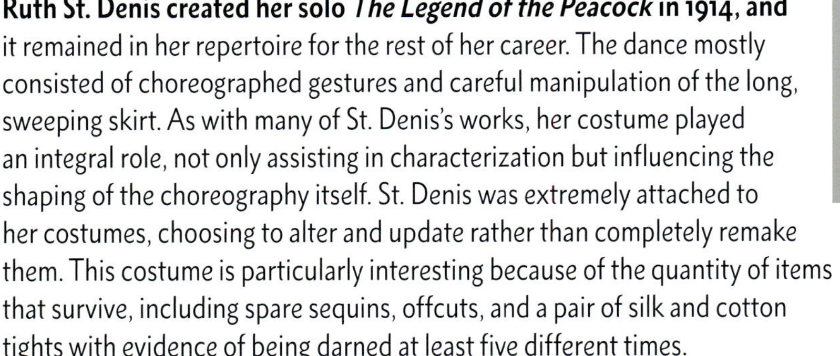

Ruth St. Denis created her solo *The Legend of the Peacock* in 1914, and it remained in her repertoire for the rest of her career. The dance mostly consisted of choreographed gestures and careful manipulation of the long, sweeping skirt. As with many of St. Denis's works, her costume played an integral role, not only assisting in characterization but influencing the shaping of the choreography itself. St. Denis was extremely attached to her costumes, choosing to alter and update rather than completely remake them. This costume is particularly interesting because of the quantity of items that survive, including spare sequins, offcuts, and a pair of silk and cotton tights with evidence of being darned at least five different times.

The bodice and skirt appear to date from 1914 and have been altered on numerous occasions. The blue cotton brocade bodice is decorated with hand-sewn rows of gelatin sequins that were later covered in a layer of plastic sequins. The hem and front closure are embellished with mirror-backed gems and decorated with loops of beads, including repurposed necklaces. The 92-inch-long skirt is made from a lime-green silk and metallic thread brocade. The current net overlay is most likely a 1920s replacement, but the peacock "eyes," in colored metal threads, appear to have been reused from the earlier version of the skirt. The sequined waistband matches the fabric and style of the bodice and shows where an extended metallic and cotton panel once was. The skirt dragged on the floor and would have been subject to a lot of wear and tear. Three iterations of the costume's plumed headdress also exist in the Jacob's Pillow Dance Festival Archives. The earliest example, now extremely fragile, is decorated with the feather plume that St. Denis allegedly plucked off a visitor's hat![1]

1. Jane Sherman, text of a lecture given at Florida State University, March 4, 1984, Jacob's Pillow Dance Festival Archives.

ABOVE LEFT
Bodice and skirt, C-001_a-b.

ABOVE RIGHT
Hand-sewn gelatin sequins on the waistband of the skirt, C-001_b.

LEFT
Metallic peacock-feather "eyes" on the train of the skirt, C-001_b.

FACING
Front closure of the skirt, C-001_b.

Nautch Dance, c. 1920

CHOREOGRAPHER
Ruth St. Denis

Choli, nautch skirt, underskirt, veil, bracelets, rings, and necklaces worn by Ruth St. Denis in *Nautch Dance*, 1920s–40s

Silk, cotton, nylon, metal, and silver

Ruth St. Denis UCLA Costume Collection, Jacob's Pillow Dance Festival Archives, C-006, 049, 053, 122_a-b, 125, 126_a-b, 129, 130, 490

Photographer not identified, *Ruth St. Denis in Nautch Costume*, not dated, photograph, $8^{13}/_{16} \times 7$ in. (22.4 × 17.8 cm). Jacob's Pillow Dance Festival Archives.

***Nautch Dance*, based on an Indian court dance, was perhaps Ruth** St. Denis's most famous work. She performed at least six distinct nautch dances across her career, including *Cadman Nautch*, *Green Nautch*, and *Palace Nautch*. St. Denis's nautch dances relied on the costume as an integral component of the choreography, perhaps more so than did any other work in her repertoire. The heavy nautch skirts sometimes contained over one hundred yards of fabric, which allowed for their swirling movement and ability to keep moving after St. Denis herself had stopped.

This particular skirt dates from the 1920s and was used by St. Denis well into the 1940s, but it is unclear for which nautch dance she wore this bright costume. She most likely bought the skirt in India in 1926. Made from approximately 32 yards of hand-printed cotton fabric, the skirt is very heavy. It gets its volume from a series of 168 darts in the material and would have been worn over several underskirts.

St. Denis wore this bodice, or choli, with the skirt in the 1940s. The bodice is made from a synthetic satin and is half green and half purple. The short sleeves are decorated with appliqués of gold embroidery that appear to have been repurposed from an older garment. The neckline and hem are edged with gold braid, and the back has an open cutout. The bodice is built over a 1940s nylon bra.

The silver jewelry worn with this costume appears also to have been purchased in India in 1926.

RIGHT
Detail of silver jewelry, C-130.

BELOW RIGHT
Arthur F. Kales (American, 1882–1936), *Ruth St. Denis "Nautch Feet,"* 1929, photograph, 10 × 8¼ in. (25.4 × 21 cm). Jacob's Pillow Dance Festival Archives.

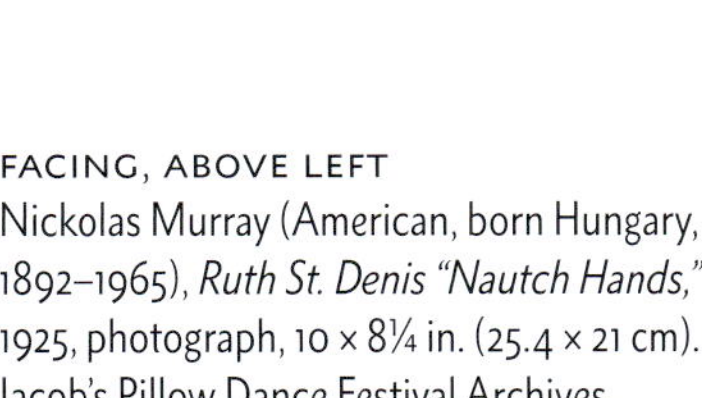

FACING, ABOVE LEFT
Nickolas Murray (American, born Hungary, 1892–1965), *Ruth St. Denis "Nautch Hands,"* 1925, photograph, 10 × 8¼ in. (25.4 × 21 cm). Jacob's Pillow Dance Festival Archives.

FACING, ABOVE RIGHT
Detail of silver bracelet and hand decoration, C-122_a-b, 126_a-b.

FACING, BELOW
Hem of the block-printed nautch skirt, C-006.

O-Mika, 1913

CHOREOGRAPHER
Ruth St. Denis

COMPOSER
Robert Hood Bowers

Kimono and obi worn by Ruth St. Denis in *O-Mika*, 1910s–20s

Silk, cotton, linen, and metal

Ruth St. Denis UCLA Costume Collection, Jacob's Pillow Dance Festival Archives, C-013, 037, 068

Photographer not identified, *Ruth St. Denis in O-Mika Costume*, not dated, photograph, $9^{15}/_{16}$ × 8 in. (24.2 × 20.32 cm). Jacob's Pillow Dance Festival Archives.

Ruth St. Denis described *O-Mika*, first created in 1913, as a "little drama with dancing interludes."[1] She performed excerpts from *O-Mika* throughout her career, reviving the whole work in the early 1960s, when this costume from the 1920s was worn once more.

This kimono dates from the mid-1920s and was possibly made for St. Denis in Japan on the Denishawn 1925–26 East and South Asian Tour. The stunning black silk kimono is decorated with two elaborately embroidered birds, one extending across the back, and flowers in a mixture of brightly colored silk and metallic threads. The kimono is lined half in red cotton and half in red silk. After the kimono was made, St. Denis had the hem padded and three additional padded sections attached on top of one another in green, yellow, and pink. Smaller padded rolls, in green, yellow, and purple, were also added to the collar and cuffs to give the impression of multiple layers. In the original choreography for *O-Mika*, St. Denis allegedly wore five kimonos under this black one. The shedding of each kimono signaled the start of a new dance and also influenced the choreography.

St. Denis wore this kimono with a black silk obi decorated with two panels of embroidery. The top panel shows a pond with a bridge and lilies stitched with colored silk and gold metallic thread. The bottom piece appears to be older and shows a dragon embroidered in metallic thread. The panels are lined with apple-green silk, and at the bottom the obi has a fringe of green silk tassels. This bottom section was originally part of an older obi that St. Denis wore in the 1910s (see fig. 3.10); the remaining fragment of this sash is also in the Ruth St. Denis UCLA Costume Collection in the Jacob's Pillow Dance Festival Archives.

1. Suzanne Shelton, *Ruth St. Denis: A Biography of the Divine Dancer* (Austin: University of Texas, 1990), 109.

Back view of kimono, C-037.

FACING, ABOVE LEFT
Front of obi showing the two panels of embroidery (bottom piece repurposed from an older costume), C-013.

FACING, ABOVE RIGHT
Detail of silk and metal embroidery on back of kimono, C-037.

FACING, BELOW
Detail of kimono showing multiple padded rolls attached to hem, C-037.

OVERLEAF
Detail of silk and metal embroidery on back of kimono, C-037.

The Costumes of Ruth St. Denis, Denishawn, and Ted Shawn and His Men Dancers

Caroline Hamilton

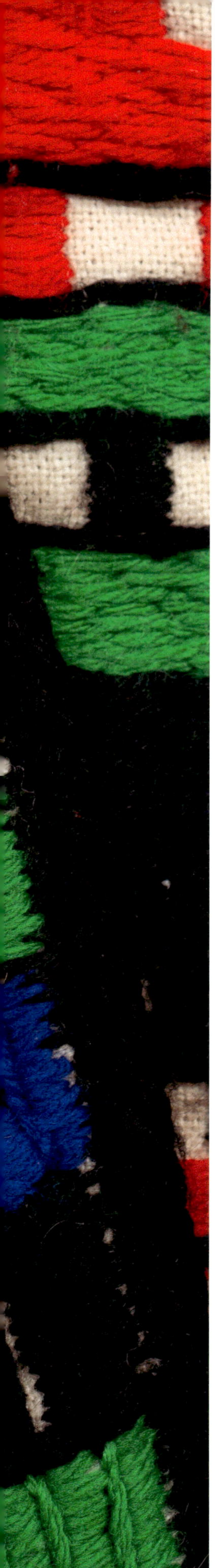

Pioneering American dancers Ruth St. Denis (1879–1968) and Ted Shawn (1891–1972) were innovators in many ways, not least in their commitment to the preservation and documentation of their art through countless photographs and an incredible wealth of moving images. Despite such enduring testimony, there is much we do not know about the dancers and their performances. However, a plethora of information can be gleaned from the surviving costumes once worn by these dancers and the members of their companies. Dance costumes are unique working garments that are often integral to the performance. Extant items can reveal details about design and construction, as well as casting, and can even provide insights into movement and choreography.

The Jacob's Pillow Costume Collection

The Jacob's Pillow Costume Collection can be grouped into four main categories: those worn by Ruth St. Denis in her solo career (approximately 1906–60s), those worn by St. Denis and Ted Shawn and the Denishawn Company (1915–31), those worn by Ted Shawn and His Men Dancers (1933–40), and, finally, smaller additions from later Jacob's Pillow productions and donations from individual dancers. These items arrived at Jacob's Pillow in stages and were initially kept not for historical reasons, but for future use.

In 1932, after the Denishawn Company had closed and St. Denis and Shawn had agreed to go their separate ways, they divided their accumulated costumes, props, and sets between them. Both kept significant items that they thought they might perhaps use again. Dancer Barton Mumaw (1912–2001), who was present when they made their selections, later recalled:

> To Siva [Shawn] went the forty pounds of silver chains, bracelets, and belts Shawn had bought in India for his *Cosmic Dance*; to the Nautch Dancer [St. Denis], her green satin, gold-bordered circular skirt, belled anklets and jewelry; to the Emperor Tepancálzin [Shawn], the enormous cape of orange feathers he had worn when partnering the young Martha Graham in *Xochitl*. Each kept those costumes in which they would perform in the years to come: her *White Jade* draperies, her *Black and Gold* sari; his *Gnossienne*, his *Thunderbird*; their *Tillers of the Soil*.[1]

After completing the division, they decided that the rest should be burned "with a cleansing fire." Those items "sacrificed" included:

> The thirty-foot-high flats representing the Babylonian god from *Ishtar of the Seven Gates*, the Hopi adobe house from *The Feather of the Dawn*, the *Spirit of the Sea* rock and fishing net and green-blue backdrop, the *Cuadro Flamenco* baskets of flowers, *Job*'s altar made of cartons, animal silhouettes from *Angkor Vat* . . . armloads of shoes and wigs, of scarves and garlands, of leotards and gauzy nautch skirts, of Egyptian masks and Viennese ball dresses.[2]

FIG. 2.1
Denishawn and Men Dancers costume and prop trunks. Jacob's Pillow Dance Festival Archives.

Shawn brought the costumes and props that he kept from the fire back to Jacob's Pillow in Becket, Massachusetts, and these selections form the nucleus of the current collection, supplemented over time with items from Shawn's Men Dancers company. As Jacob's Pillow Director of Preservation Norton Owen notes, "The Denishawn costumes had to be brought here, but in a way the Men Dancers costumes were born here,"[3] with the majority, in fact, being made at the Pillow.

The blue-and-yellow-banded Denishawn trunks and Men Dancers traveling trunks (fig. 2.1) continued to house these costumes, which were stored in various buildings and loft spaces around the Pillow grounds. Some of them were used by students over the years, but the majority lay dormant.

FIG. 2.2
Black and gold nautch costume worn by Ruth St. Denis, 1910s, photographed on the Tea Garden platform, Jacob's Pillow, 1977. Jacob's Pillow Dance Festival Archives.

FIG. 2.3
Unidentified Chinese robe, c. 1920s, photographed on the Tea Garden platform, Jacob's Pillow, 1977. Jacob's Pillow Dance Festival Archives.

In 1977, Owen, who was working as a box office assistant at the time, created a small, temporary display of costumes at the Pillow, using mannequins borrowed from a Pittsfield, Massachusetts, department store (figs. 2.2 and 2.3). While this was more than a dozen years before Owen was formally entrusted with the Pillow Archives, it was an important turning point and marks the first time any of the costumes were exhibited.

Opening the Trunks

In the summer of 1981, Owen undertook an inventory of a large number of the trunks, together with Jacob's Pillow resident costume designer Charles "Chip" Schoonmaker, assisted by Barton Mumaw and former Denishawn dancer Jane Sherman (1908–2010). They carried the trunks outside and spread the contents onto sheets, grouped items together, made detailed descriptions and illustrations, and took Polaroids of the objects (figs. 2.4 and 2.5). They recorded any names found inside the costumes and made attributions wherever possible.

The following year, the Berkshire Museum invited Jacob's Pillow to create an exhibition. Owen chose a small range of costume items to display, including some made for Shawn. After this exhibition, they went back into the trunks and into storage around the Jacob's Pillow campus. Then, in 1990, Owen was approached to curate *Ted Shawn: A Centennial Tribute to the Father of American Dance* for the National Museum of Dance in Saratoga Springs, New York.

FIG. 2.4
Wrap and manta from *The Feather of the Dawn*, 1923, Polaroids from the 1981 inventory of the Jacob's Pillow Costume Collection. Jacob's Pillow Dance Festival Archives.

FIG. 2.5
Barton Mumaw trying on the wig from *Momiji-Gari*, 1926, that was made for Ted Shawn in Japan, Polaroid from the 1981 inventory of the Jacob's Pillow Costume Collection. Jacob's Pillow Dance Festival Archives.

FIG. 2.6
Jeweled velvet tunic worn by Ted Shawn for *The Siamese Ballet*, 1922, designed by Pearl Wheeler; silk, cotton, metal, glass. Ted Shawn Costume Collection, Jacob's Pillow Dance Festival Archives, C-545_a-g.

It was so successful it ran for two seasons, from May 1991 to October 1992. That exhibition featured key examples from Shawn's career, including costumes from *Cuadro Flamenco* (see p. 46), *Valse Directoire*, and *The Siamese Ballet* (fig. 2.6).

In the mid-1990s, the trunks were moved in stages to the basement of Blake's Barn, home of the Jacob's Pillow Dance Festival Archives, on the Pillow campus, where they would be in a more stable climate. The Dance Department at the University of California, Los Angeles (UCLA), donated a second collection of costumes to Jacob's Pillow in 2000. Originally a gift from Ruth St. Denis to UCLA in the 1960s, the collection comprises the costumes she had kept after the division with Shawn in 1932 and later additions from her solo career.

FIG. 2.7
Headdress worn in *Angkor Vat*, 1930, made by Lester Shafer after designs by Pearl Wheeler; cotton, paper, wood, metal. Ruth St. Denis UCLA Costume Collection, Jacob's Pillow Dance Festival Archives, C-011.

Prominent works from her repertoire represented in this collection include *Angkor Vat* (fig. 2.7), *The Cobras*, *The Dance of Theodora*, *The Incense*, *Kwan Yin*, *The Legend of the Peacock* (see p. 20), *Nautch Dance* (see p. 24), *O-Mika* (see p. 28), *Radha* (see figs. 3.4, 4.8), and *Valse Directoire*. In 2018, the combined Jacob's Pillow Costume Collection, numbering some 2,500 costume and prop items, was catalogued and rehoused. The earliest costume identified, worn by St. Denis in *The Cobras*, dates from 1906; the most recent costumes, made for the Jacob's Pillow production of *The Mountain Whippoorwill*, date from 1964.

While the Jacob's Pillow Costume Collection comprises the majority of surviving costumes from Ruth St. Denis, Denishawn, and Ted Shawn and His Men Dancers, there is another, smaller collection at Florida State University. It includes additional costumes used and owned by Shawn that had been stored in Florida, and in some cases contains the other half of costume sets housed at Jacob's Pillow. Pam and Charles Killinger acquired the collection in the summer of 1983 at the Florida estate auction of John Christian (1921–1982), Shawn's partner and former director of Jacob's Pillow. The couple then donated the approximately four hundred items to the Florida State University Department of Dance. Pam Killinger later wrote: "I was afraid that if he [the auctioneer] acquired the collection it would be sold off piece-by-piece, perhaps to people who didn't even understand its significance to dance history, but who just wanted an interesting trinket to place on a mantlepiece or coffee table."[4]

Designing and Making the Costumes of Ted Shawn and Ruth St. Denis

Dance costumes must work with a dancer to allow movement—or not—according to the choreography, and must also reflect the intent of the work. Dance costumes are made to have a life of up to several years (sometimes decades) and often need to accommodate multiple wearers. A costume that fits and moves well can make a performance, becoming a dancer's partner. For St. Denis and Shawn, costumes were a crucial aspect of their work. A Denishawn School prospectus from the 1920s declared that all costumes were "built on the fundamental lines of truth and beauty."[5]

Sherman described the costuming for the Denishawn company "either as an essential adjunct or as the actual stimulus or reason for a dance."[6] For many of the dances, the costume was indeed the driving force, in particular for St. Denis. She and Shawn undertook extensive research when creating new works and would often purchase traditional garments to replicate for stage costumes. Dancer Barton Mumaw recalled in 1984: "Many of the dances of Denishawn were based upon, or inspired by, National and ethnic forms and so far as possible authentically dressed, not only to give the quality of movement suitable to the subject but also because the costumes shaped the motions of the human body."[7]

While Shawn and St. Denis often incorporated "authentic" garments into their stage apparel, they also had the ability to see the theatrical potential in any manner of items. They very rarely employed designers, preferring to create their costumes organically, and wherever they traveled would go searching for

things they could perform in. Shawn described in his biography that "sales girls at jewelry counters would be suspicious of Ruth who looked like a storybook schoolmarm and acted like a dime-novel madam . . . wearing a prim tailored suit and plain felt hat." She would "paw through junk gems, trying on the flashiest of rings, earrings, and pins."[8] When Shawn required a new headdress for one of his works, he thought a kitchen colander would be the thing:

FIG. 2.8
Albert Witzel (American, 1879–1929), *Pearl Wheeler*, 1922, photograph, 10 × 8 in. (24.4 × 20.32 cm). Jacob's Pillow Dance Festival Archives.

> I wandered around a kitchenware department trying on colanders saying to the salesgirl, "Don't you have a colander, size seven and a quarter? None of these fit." Just in time I found the right size and escaped to the toy department where I bought a tin horn to make the spire-shaped top of the royal headgear. With tin shears, a couple of filigree metal lampshades and long needles, I produced a crown that survived many seasons of one-night stands.[9]

The ideas came from St. Denis and Shawn, but someone still needed to create the physical costumes. Determining who made them in the early days of St. Denis's solo career and then for Denishawn is an ongoing research project, but we know that in 1917–18, the Denishawn workshop was run by Grace Ripley, a well-known costumier from Boston. During Ripley's running of the Denishawn costume shop, "a girl came one day, offering to join her sewing class if only she might somehow join the dancing class as well."[10] This "girl" was Pearl Wheeler (1884–1963), who, as St. Denis later explained, would "became part of the cement of that structure called Denishawn" (fig. 2.8).[11] Wheeler did go on to dance briefly with the company, but her real talents lay in her ability to realize the fantastical creations devised by Shawn and St. Denis. Sherman recalled that "for more than fifteen years," Wheeler "translated the ideas of St. Denis and Shawn into reality, frequently contributing her own invaluable thoughts not only to the choice of material and style but even to the choreography of those of Miss Ruth's solos which depended upon line, fabric, and color for the maximum effectiveness" (fig. 2.9).[12]

Wheeler worked as wardrobe mistress as well as dresser and companion to St. Denis until the Denishawn company's closure in the early 1930s. A 1965 tribute to Wheeler by John Dougherty in *Dance Magazine* described the basement "costume room" at New York's Denishawn House:

> It was Pearl's domain, not to be entered without her invitation . . . large, battered, henna-colored touring trunks lined the walls, and out of them spilled all the color and exotic excitement of an East Indian bazaar. . . .
>
> All the material necessary for new costumes—bolts of cloth, rolls of braid, boxes of buttons, trimmings of all kinds were stacked on shelves within reach of the sewing tables. Close to Pearl's sewing machine was a dressmaker's dummy adjusted to St. Denis's measurements-of-the-moment.[13]

By the 1930s, the requirements of dance costumes were changing. Those for the Men Dancers company reflect Shawn's shifting values and priorities as a choreographer. His new focus on the athletic and abstract demanded garments that allowed the movements of the body to be shown. Costumes remained, however, just as integral to the Men Dancers' performances as they had been to those of Denishawn. The 1930s also brought changes beyond stylistic concerns. The nationwide depression required that cheap and effective costume solutions be found. Shawn was skilled at seeing the potential in items, just as he had envisioned a humble colander becoming an elaborate headdress. With a limited budget, he now adapted swim trunks, store-bought shirts, and sweaters into costumes for his Men Dancers.

For St. Denis and Shawn during the days of Denishawn, a costume would often dictate a work; now the choreography and movement led the way. Mumaw recalled that new works at Jacob's Pillow initially were "performed in practice clothes and simulated props and accessories to get the reaction of the audience and critics. Shawn used to say the dances had to stand on movement alone before they were worthy of time and money being spent on them."[14]

Shawn and former Men Dancer George Horn (1911–1961) designed the costumes for the Men Dancers (see pp. 98–101), and Horn made the majority

FIG. 2.9
Silk dress and armbands worn by Ruth St. Denis in the role of Isis in *The Egyptian Ballet*, 1920s, silk, cotton, elastic, metal. Ted Shawn Costume Collection, Jacob's Pillow Dance Festival Archives, C-547_a-d.

of them using a treadle Singer sewing machine nicknamed "ziggurat." For the finer sewing and tailoring, he had help from Hattie Sherman, who had previously worked for Denishawn under Pearl Wheeler. Mumaw later wrote:

> Hattie knew all about the strain that dancing places upon fabrics that must nevertheless keep their shape. We welcomed her into the family. I doubt if she had ever been out of New York before, but she showed no disdain for the primitive living conditions of the Farm [Jacob's Pillow], or any fear of the open spaces that surrounded it. Professional though she was in her craft, Hattie drew the line at one thing: she insisted that George do the fitting of our costume G-strings.[15]

Conclusion

The survival of the costumes at Jacob's Pillow provides a unique window into how these companies were run and how their productions looked. Complete costume outfits, as well as full-company sets and multiple iterations of some costumes, provide an unprecedented insight into the evolution of certain dances. Much of this information is unavailable from any other surviving sources. The Jacob's Pillow Costume Collection is an important resource for both current and future scholarship on early modern dance and the evolution of dance costume and design.

Notes

1. Barton Mumaw and Jane Sherman, *Barton Mumaw, Dancer: From Denishawn to Jacob's Pillow and Beyond* (New York: Dance Horizons, 1986), 63–65.

2. Mumaw and Sherman, *Barton Mumaw, Dancer*, 63–65.

3. Norton Owen, oral history interview by Caroline Hamilton, February 2, 2018, video recording, Jacob's Pillow Dance Festival Archives.

4. Pam Killinger, quoted in Tricia Henry Young, *The Killinger Collection: Costumes of Denishawn and Ted Shawn and His Men Dancers* (Tallahassee: Florida State University Department of Dance, 1999), 5.

5. 1920s prospectus for the Denishawn School, Jacob's Pillow Dance Festival Archives.

6. Jane Sherman, *The Drama of Denishawn Dance* (Middletown, CT: Wesleyan University Press, 1979), 11.

7. Barton Mumaw, "Costume: Ruth St. Denis, Ted Shawn, Men Dancers," lecture notes, Spring 1984, 189.43, p. 3, Barton Mumaw Collection, Jacob's Pillow Dance Festival Archives.

8. Ted Shawn, *One Thousand and One Night Stands* (Garden City, NY: Doubleday, 1960), 68.

9. Shawn, *One Thousand and One Nights Stands*, 69.

10. Ruth St. Denis, *An Unfinished Life: An Autobiography* (New York: Harper, 1939), 201.

11. St. Denis, *An Unfinished Life*, 201.

12. Sherman, *Drama of Denishawn Dance*, 11–12.

13. John Dougherty, "Pearl Wheeler: A Tribute," *Dance Magazine*, January 1965, 53.

14. Mumaw, "Costume," 4.

15. Mumaw and Sherman, *Barton Mumaw, Dancer*, 106.

Cuadro Flamenco, 1923

COMPANY
Denishawn

CHOREOGRAPHER
Ted Shawn

COMPOSER
Louis Horst after traditional Spanish dance and music

DESIGNER
Ted Shawn and Pearl Wheeler

MAKER
Antonio R. Manfredi, Seville

Traje de luces (suit of lights) worn by Ted Shawn in the role of Lalanda in *Cuadro Flamenco*, made c. 1910

Silk, cotton, metal, glass, and wood

Ted Shawn Costume Collection, Jacob's Pillow Dance Festival Archives, C-546_a-d

White Studio, New York (American, 1903–1939), *Ted Shawn*, 1923, photograph, 9¾ x 7¾ in. (24.8 x 19.7 cm). Jacob's Pillow Dance Festival Archives.

Ted Shawn purchased this traditional *traje de luces* bullfighter costume in Seville in 1923. While visiting Spain, Shawn began planning a new work titled *Cuadro Flamenco*. He took dance lessons wherever he could and began sourcing authentic props and costumes.

This suit appears to have been made by renowned "tailor of toreadors" Antonio Manfredi and was bought secondhand by Shawn. The original owner of the suit had been gored in the leg (with evidence of this in the neat patch on the left leg) and was superstitious about wearing the outfit again. The bright-green costume was later publicized as having been owned by famed bullfighter José Gómez Ortega (1895–1920), known as El Gallito or Joselito.[1] "The green suit," Shawn recalled, "was so loaded with gold thread and sequins that I staggered under its weight."[2] Shawn was able to buy the complete outfit, which included "cape, jacket, vest, pants, hat, girdle, and pigtail complete with rubber band to hold it on."[3]

The fitted jacket is made of green silk satin lined with cotton, and the surface is heavily embroidered with metallic sequins and thread. The matching high-waisted breeches are made of green silk jersey and have appliquéd panels of green silk embroidered with metallic sequins and thread on each thigh. Although the vest, girdle, and pigtail that Shawn originally purchased are no longer with the collection, the original astrakhan montera hat and cape remain. The cape is made of bright-purple silk and is also decorated with metal sequins and metallic embroidery. A label inside the montera reads: "Antonio Manfredi, Quintana 15, Sevilla."

1. "Uniform of Bull-Fighter Who Was Gored to Be Worn by Ted Shawn Here," *Bismarck Tribune*, November 22, 1924.

2. Ted Shawn, *One Thousand and One Night Stands* (Garden City, NY: Doubleday, 1960), 134.

3. Shawn, *One Thousand and One Night Stands*, 134.

RIGHT
Detail showing metal work and decoration on shoulder of jacket, C-546_a.

OVERLEAF
Back of green silk jacket, C-546_a.

FACING
Detail showing repair in leg of breeches, where original owner was gored, C-546_b.

The Feather of the Dawn, 1923

COMPANY
Denishawn

CHOREOGRAPHER
Ted Shawn

COMPOSER
Charles Wakefield Cadman based on Native American airs

DESIGNER
Earle Franke

Manta worn by Ernestine Day and Louise Brooks in the role of Kodeh; briefs, loincloth, belt, and necklace worn by Ted Shawn in the role of Kwahu, in *The Feather of the Dawn*, 1923

Wool, cotton, metal fastenings, leather, silver, turquoise

Ted Shawn Costume Collection, Jacob's Pillow Dance Festival Archives, C-161_2, 163, 164_a-c

White Studio, New York (American, 1903–1939), *Denishawn Performing The Feather of the Dawn*, Ted Shawn as Kwahu at center and Louise Brooks as Kodeh at far right, 1923, photograph, 7¾ × 9¾ in. (19.7 × 24.8 cm). Jacob's Pillow Dance Festival Archives.

The Feather of the Dawn **was the** first ensemble work in Denishawn's repertoire with a Native American theme. Taking choreographic inspiration from the Hopi, Ted Shawn bought a number of genuine Native American garments, which designer Earle Franke and costume maker Pearl Wheeler then adapted into costumes or copied.

This dress, or manta, was worn by both Ernestine Day and Louise Brooks in the role of Kodeh. The costume appears to have been altered and adapted from two traditional handwoven and embroidered mantas. This one-shoulder wool dress is decorated with thick wool embroidery around the neckline, waist, and bottom half of the skirt. It has hook-and-bar fastenings down one side. The other female characters wore copies of this garment made from painted cotton.

Shawn's costume for the role of Kwahu also contains traditional elements that Shawn had purchased. The wool wrap, like Kodeh's manta, has been adapted with theatrical fastenings for use on stage. The wrap is completely hand sewn and embroidered with panels representing clouds and rain along with other designs symbolic of nature. Elements of this costume, including the high-cut red wool briefs, heavy leather belt decorated with silver and turquoise, and silver squash-blossom necklace, can also be seen in Albert Herter's portrait of Shawn (see fig. 3.1).

ABOVE LEFT
Hand embroidery on loincloth for the role of Kwahu, C-161_2.

ABOVE RIGHT
Detail from silver, turquoise, and leather belt for the role of Kwahu, C-164_b.

LEFT
Side closure of manta for the role of Kodeh, C-163.

FACING
Hand embroidery on hem of manta for the role of Kodeh, C-163.

Water Movement, from Dance of the Ages, 1938

COMPANY
Ted Shawn and His Men Dancers

CHOREOGRAPHER
Ted Shawn

COMPOSER
Jess Meeker

MAKER
Aldrich & Aldrich, Chicago

Shapiro Studios, Pittsfield, Massachusetts (American, c. 1929–1976), *Ted Shawn and Men Dancers Performing the Water Movement from Dance of the Ages at Jacob's Pillow*, c. 1938, photograph, 8 × 9⅞ in. (20.3 × 25.1 cm). Jacob's Pillow Dance Festival Archives.

Label inside leotard, C-264.

Leotard worn by Ted Shawn in the role of the Poet-Philosopher in "Movement Quality Based on the Element of Water," from *Dance of the Ages*, 1938

Rayon, silk, cotton, metal fastenings

Ted Shawn Costume Collection, Jacob's Pillow Dance Festival Archives, C-264

This long-sleeved blue leotard with appliquéd panels of hand-painted silk crêpe de chine was made for Ted Shawn in his role of the Poet-Philosopher in the "Movement Quality Based on the Element of Water" from the full-length work *Dance of the Ages*. This is the second costume Shawn had made for this role, the first being a plain-colored leotard. This second leotard is made from a rayon knit with limited stretch, requiring it to be fastened by a long row of hooks and bars up the center back; it has a waistband inside to assist in retaining the costume's shape. The leotard was made for Shawn by athletic-wear makers Aldrich & Aldrich, Chicago, and contains Shawn's measurements inside:

> 920 T. Shawn
> 36 / 31 / 39 / 20
> 22 ½" / 44 ½" / 5'11

The Ted Shawn Costume Collection at Jacob's Pillow houses multiple sets of costumes from *Dance of the Ages* showing the evolution of the work. The first set of costumes from the Earth movement are jumpsuits and tops that were designed to look like a full bodysuit, but due to the lack of stretch in the fabric had to be made in two parts. When the work was revived the following year, Aldrich & Aldrich made a new set of Earth jumpsuits in a synthetic stretch, as well as a new set of Water movement costumes, including this leotard. The first set of trousers for Water were made from raw silk noil, whereas the second set are made from a green stretch fabric and very low cut. Each of the new outfits contains a label with the exact measurements of the intended dancer.

The costumes in the Jacob's Pillow Costume Collection represent not only the evolution of modern dance but also the changing aesthetics of and requirements for dance attire as choreography became more athletic.

The Artistic Collaborations and Cultural Appropriations

of Ruth St. Denis and Ted Shawn

Kevin M. Murphy

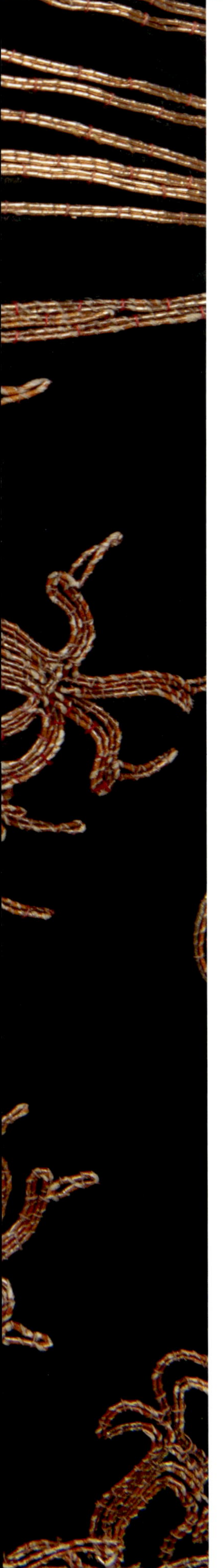

American dance icons Ruth St. Denis (1879–1968) and Ted Shawn (1891–1972) collaborated with visual artists to create images that span from the traditional to the avant-garde. They were both opportunistic and inclusive in forming relationships with artists, but their aesthetics—in dance and the visual arts—remained grounded largely in the late nineteenth century. Their collaborations included mutually beneficial partnerships with European and US painters, sculptors, and photographers, but also choreography drawing on the unacknowledged labor of Indigenous and non-Western artists and performers from around the world, complicating the legacies of Shawn and St. Denis, and the history of American modern dance.

As a child, St. Denis's mother introduced her to metaphysically informed movement techniques circulating in the United States during the late nineteenth century, most notably those of François Delsarte (1811–1871), who believed that physical actions corresponded to spiritual acts. Beginning as a teenager, St. Denis performed on vaudeville and Broadway stages, as a soloist and in companies. In 1906, she synthesized her interests in spirituality, dance, and South Asian cultures to create *Radha*, the first of many solo dances on Orientalist themes. These works propelled her to worldwide stardom, and she is considered a foundational modern dancer, along with Isadora Duncan (1877–1927) and Loie Fuller (1862–1928). Ted Shawn saw St. Denis perform in 1911, which became a transformative experience for his life and career. He had recently started dancing as physical therapy after an illness, and by 1913 he was working as a professional dancer and teacher in Los Angeles. Shawn and St. Denis met and married in 1914, and they founded Denishawn (1915–30), the first important dance company in the United States and the first to tour Asia. Denishawn—and the couple's marriage and professional partnership—ended in 1931, after several years of turmoil that included affairs and separate performing tours. By that time, St. Denis's solo work was considered old fashioned, supplanted by the formalist Modernism of her former students and Denishawn company members Martha Graham (1894–1991), Doris Humphrey (1895–1958), and Charles Weidman (1901–1975). Shawn, on the other hand, thrived after the end of Denishawn, founding Ted Shawn and His Men Dancers (1933–40), the first company of exclusively male-identified performers. He also started the Jacob's Pillow Dance Festival in Western Massachusetts, which remains an important venue for dance in the United States. From the earliest days of the festival in the 1940s, Shawn invited companies from around the world, as well as African American and Indigenous American dancers, to perform and teach at Jacob's Pillow, introducing audiences to dance and cultural forms that St. Denis and Shawn had frequently appropriated throughout their careers as dancers and choreographers. He also often invited St. Denis to Jacob's Pillow, helping to revive her career and cement her status as one of the most important contributors to the development of modern dance.

St. Denis's and Shawn's choreography often relied on the visual arts. St. Denis characterized her approach to dance as optical rather than musical, and artworks helped shape the performances she created. Indeed, her origin story famously recounts how an illustrator's rendering of the Egyptian goddess Isis on a cigarette advertisement inspired St. Denis to imbue her dances with spiritual intent.[1] Subsequently, many of her, and Denishawn's, pieces were based on works St. Denis studied in museums, including New York's Metropolitan Museum of Art and the British Museum in London.[2]

Paintings, drawings, and portrait photographs depicting Shawn and St. Denis, in turn, join the rich material culture of Denishawn and the Men Dancers—including spectacular costumes along with thousands of documentary photographs, pamphlets, programs, magazines, and other ephemera—much of it held by the Jacob's Pillow Dance Festival Archives. Although both St. Denis and Shawn were heavily invested in shaping their image throughout their careers, and the archives today hold a trove of documents and artifacts for research, the art and material culture surrounding St. Denis and Shawn has been hitherto little studied. (By contrast, the art and artistic collaborations of the European Modernist Ballets Russes, which also has a legacy of cultural appropriation and is perhaps the closest analogue to Denishawn, are well documented in art and dance history, including several museum exhibitions.[3]) The artworks and artifacts associated with St. Denis and Shawn are important for understanding the early history of modern dance in the United States and the international communities of artists and dancers to which they belonged. Connections between dancers and the visual arts also provide a lens to interrogate the history of Modernism in the United States, especially the overlooked role that dancers played in it.

Many of the visual artists who collaborated with the pair during their partnership running Denishawn occupy a liminal space within the history of modern art—just as St. Denis and Shawn do in modern dance—making work that is somewhat Modernist but lacking many formal markers of the truly modern. St. Denis, for example, modeled for sculptors Auguste Rodin and Gaston Lachaise, who remained grounded in the human figure but exaggerated it to convey movement and expression. Academically trained American artist Albert Herter painted life-size portraits of both St. Denis and Shawn in the bright colors and loose handling of paint associated with proto-modern Impressionism. The couple were also interested in the antimodern Arts and Crafts movement and tried to incorporate the movement's ideas about valorizing craft and integrating different artistic disciplines into Denishawn. However, after the company's dissolution, Shawn found himself in the artistic circle of the Société Anonyme, Inc., an organization that championed

Modernism in America, led by the Dadaist Marcel Duchamp, the Surrealist Man Ray, and the artist and patron Katherine Dreier. Portraits of Shawn and promotional materials for his solo career and new company, Ted Shawn and His Men Dancers, reveal the aesthetic influences of Cubism, Futurism, and geometric abstraction, coinciding with his move toward more abstract choreography.

In drawing inspiration from the visual and performing arts, the pair also borrowed heavily from non-Western traditions, looking most often at the art and dance of Egypt, Morocco, China, Japan, India, and other South and East Asian cultures. Shawn became enamored with dances by Indigenous Americans, particularly from the Hopi Tribe. While their collaborations with Western artists were equally beneficial, as both artists and dancers used the resulting images for publicity, their borrowings from non-Western and Indigenous American sources served only St. Denis's and Shawn's careers. What we now understand to be St. Denis's and Shawn's practice of Orientalist cultural appropriation resulted from their viewing and appreciating dance from around the world. While their admiration for their source material was genuine, it was inseparable from the settler-colonialist ideologies they absorbed as Anglo-Americans born in the late nineteenth century. Beyond simply adopting aesthetics and techniques from other cultures, they frequently portrayed characters from a range of nonwhite communities. From a twenty-first-century perspective, regardless of their intent, Shawn and St. Denis were white dancers who became celebrities by using their privilege to pretend to be people of color.

In pursuit of authenticity, St. Denis and Shawn sought dance lessons from native practitioners at home and abroad. St. Denis created her breakthrough *Radha*, which debuted in 1906, by observing Indian performers at the World's Columbian Exposition in Chicago in 1893 and at Coney Island, as well as by learning from members of Indian communities in New York. For performances of her "East Indian" series, encompassing *Radha*, *The Incense*, and *The Cobras*, St. Denis hired Indian nationals for supporting—and subservient—roles as priests, musicians, or street buskers (see fig. 4.8). In performances of *Radha*, the Indians on stage were perhaps those who had helped teach her Indian dance, yet they received no credit or mention for their contributions. Dance historian Priya Srinivasan writes that the Indian men with her "could only ever serve St. Denis, onstage and off, as laborers. It was their very labor that was effaced by St. Denis and masqueraded as her labor."[4]

Shawn, for his part, benefited from the cultural labor of Native Americans. He saw in their rituals an opportunity for him to create an authentically American form of dance, separate from European traditions, and to foreground male dancers.[5] He had created his first dance on Indigenous American themes in 1917, and he wears American Indian costumes in many iconic images, including the monumental portrait by Albert Herter from 1925 (fig. 3.1). In a 1923 photograph by the New York–based White Studio (fig. 3.2), Shawn is portrayed sitting pensively with kachinas at his feet, in costume for his Hopi-influenced *The Feather of the Dawn* (see p. 52), an evening-length program that debuted that year. In the figure's contemplative pose, the props, and use of sepia tone,

FIG. 3.1, FACING
Albert Herter (American, 1871–1950), *Ted Shawn*, 1925, oil on canvas, 96 × 46 in. (243.8 × 116.8 cm). Jacob's Pillow Dance Festival Archives.

FIG. 3.2
White Studio, New York (1903–1939), *Ted Shawn in Costume for The Feather of the Dawn*, 1923, photograph, 10⅞ × 13⅞ in. (27.6 × 35.2 cm). Jacob's Pillow Dance Festival Archives.

the photo resembles contemporaneous photographs by Edward S. Curtis, who documented Indigenous people throughout the United States over thirty years. Like Curtis in his highly staged, ahistorical portraits, the White Studio presented Shawn "playing Indian," as if Native Americans lived in a place where their cultural traditions remained untouched by the violence enacted on them since colonists arrived in the Americas.

The photograph was part of the promotional campaign for *The Feather of the Dawn*. Shawn based the set design on the Walpi Pueblo in Arizona, and the principal dancers, including Shawn, wore Native-made textiles and jewelry recut and repurposed as costumes (see fig. 4.11). Corps dancers' costumes were decorated with Hopi textile motifs, and some dancers wore kachina head pieces that the production's designer, Earle Franke, copied directly from a book published by the Smithsonian Institution in 1904. The work included eight dances inspired by ceremonies Shawn had seen in the Southwest as well as by his research in museums and libraries.[6]

Shawn created *The Feather of the Dawn* as Pueblo communities resisted whites commodifying their ceremonial dances. In 1913, the Hopi at Walpi banned photography and filming of the Snake Dance, and by the late 1920s, they had expanded the ban to all their ceremonies.[7] Shawn knew that the Hopi did not want their culture commercialized, but he dismissed this as "prejudice and superstition."[8] According to Shawn's biographer Paul Scolieri, "in restaging a katchinas [*sic*] dance, Shawn sought to capitalize on the ban by providing a live action reenactment of the ceremony, despite the prohibitions. . . . Shawn's pursuit of ethnic, national, and racial dances was surely economic."[9]

Through their sustained practice of appropriation, St. Denis and Shawn profited from American and European interest in the religious and artistic achievements of other cultures, some of which had been subjugated as colonies by Western nations.[10] Their access, through museums, to the objects that inspired their work was often made possible by European and Anglo-American plundering of cultural artifacts. They also used their privileged position to study dance from members of the cultures they became interested in, usually without crediting their instructors' labor. The couple had very different relationships with visual artists in the United States and Europe. Images of St. Denis and Shawn in costume by these artists reinforced colonial and racist political, social, and economic practices, while elevating their status as performers and celebrities. While they should not be expected to have rejected the prejudices of their time, their work contributes to a continuing legacy of harmful and racist appropriation in dance.

The Early Years: Ruth St. Denis

Ruth St. Denis spent her early career as a solo performer first on the dime museum and vaudeville circuits, and then as an actress and dancer in Broadway productions.[11] Violet Oakley's drawings of St. Denis from this period concentrate on her arms, the sinuous movement of which would become her signature, and voluminous drapery she manipulated expressively (fig. 3.3). At the time, Oakley was primarily working as an illustrator, but she would soon become one of the few women who created large-scale murals for public and private buildings, including the United States Capitol. Both Oakley and St. Denis were Christian Scientists.[12] When St. Denis achieved fame with *Radha*, playing the titular Hindu goddess and consort to Krishna, she was recognized as a fine artist, performing concert dance, rather than a mere entertainer of suspect morals wearing scandalous costumes. She explored the senses of sight, hearing, taste, and smell, becoming delirious with physical pleasure. However, by the end of the dance, she rejected the sensual in favor of the spiritual. Performing in bare legs and arms with an exposed midriff, while covered in skin darkening makeup, St. Denis exuded sexuality yet rebuffed it through the spiritual themes of the dance.[13] Her association with elite women, many of whom—including art collector and museum founder Isabella Stewart Gardner—had connections to the visual arts, also helped legitimize St. Denis as a dancer of higher truth.[14]

In a luminous pastel, American illustrator Harper Pennington portrayed St. Denis dancing *Radha* at the home of Boston socialite Marian Appleton Coolidge (fig. 3.4). More effectively than the black-and-white photography of the time could have done, Pennington's Impressionistic style, influenced by James Abbott MacNeil Whistler, indicates how *Radha* would have entranced audiences. St. Denis emerges from a tonally unified background of dark red, in mid-turn, with her arms spread dramatically and her skirt swirling around her. Pennington added small areas of color and white highlights to the composition, suggesting the dazzling effect of theatrical lighting on her reflective costume. St. Denis became renowned for her stagecraft, and Pennington's pastel demonstrates that

FIG. 3.3, BELOW
Violet Oakley (American, 1874–1961), *Ruth St. Denis*, c. 1905, charcoal and chalk on paper, $22\frac{1}{4} \times 15\frac{3}{8}$ in. (31.4 × 23.4 cm). National Portrait Gallery, Smithsonian Institution; Gift of the Violet Oakley Memorial Foundation, NPG.83.19.

FIG. 3.4, FACING
Harper Pennington (American, 1854–1920), *Ruth St. Denis in Radha*, 1906, pastel on paper, $11\frac{3}{4} \times 5\frac{1}{2}$ in. (29.8 × 14 cm). Jacob's Pillow Dance Festival Archives; Donated by Donna Brent.

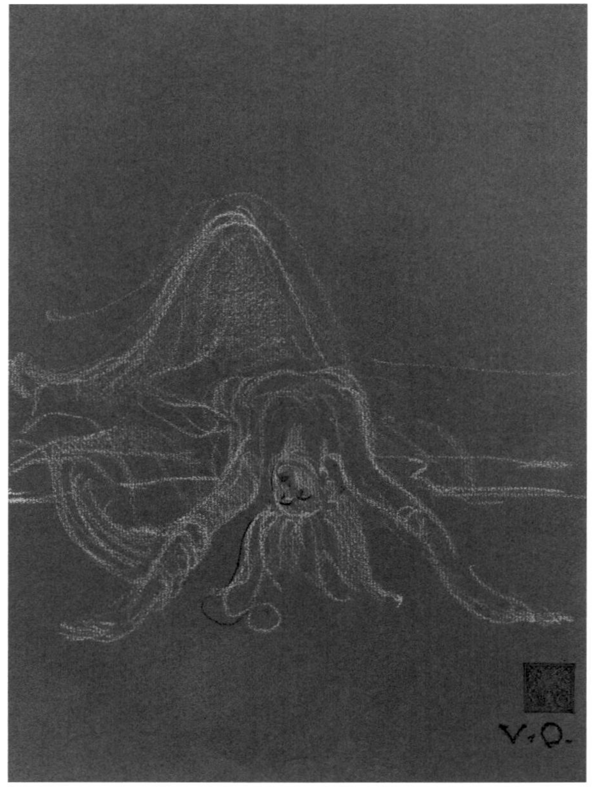

from early in her career, the dancer paid close attention to how costuming and lighting enhanced her choreography.

St. Denis began performing *Radha* and a new dance, *The Cobras*, at theaters in New York, becoming one of America's first dance celebrities, along with Isadora Duncan and Loie Fuller. Like them, St. Denis also left the United States to tour Europe, where concert dance was better established. She performed in Britain, France, Germany, Austria, Czechoslovakia (now the Czech Republic), and Hungary beginning in the fall of 1906 and returned to the United States in 1909.

While abroad, St. Denis danced and modeled for several artists, including the Anglo-Dutch painter Lawrence Alma-Tadema, the French sculptor Auguste Rodin, and the American expatriate John Singer Sargent. Rodin made around a dozen sketches of St. Denis in 1906, including *Femme nue de dos, à mi-corps et bras ouverts dite la danseuse Ruth* (*Nude Woman from the Back, Half-Length with Open Arms, Known as the Dancer Ruth*) (fig. 3.5). The art historian Juliet Bellow has argued that the nascent modern dance movement and Modernism in other visual arts had a mutually beneficial relationship. Dancers elevated their status in high culture through association with established artists, while painters and sculptors looked to dance for abstract modes of expression and entrepreneurial models for marketing their work independently, outside of official state institutions.[15]

In his images of St. Denis, Rodin emphasized the energetic motion of her arms and torso, which may have influenced his own approach to depicting the dynamic relationship of the body with space.[16] This focus on the dancer's

FIG. 3.5
Auguste Rodin (French, 1840–1917), *Femme nue de dos, à mi-corps et bras ouverts dite la danseuse Ruth* (*Nude Woman from the Back, Half-Length with Open Arms, Known as the Dancer Ruth*), c. 1907, graphite on paper, 7⅞ × 12⅛ in. (20.1 × 30.9 cm). Musée Rodin, Paris, D.05693.

arms may have derived from St. Denis manipulating her arms and hands to create the illusion of cobras moving hypnotically to a snake charmer's flute in *The Cobras*. At the climax of the performance, St. Denis's cobra-hands would suddenly strike at the audience.

German artist Leo Rauth featured an image of St. Denis performing *The Cobras* in a portfolio of pochoir prints (fig. 3.6). Unlike Rodin—and other artists who portrayed St. Denis at climactic moments of her choreography—Rauth depicted St. Denis at the beginning of the dance with her arms and costume gathered close to her body, the "snakes" coiled around her. Rauth also made St. Denis extremely thin, the ideal body type for dancers in Europe at the time, and with her back slightly bent, so that her body describes a gentle and elegant S-curve. Rauth's image closely resembles a carte de visite of St. Denis in *The Cobras*, such that one may have influenced the other.

After St. Denis returned to the United States, the French-born sculptor Gaston Lachaise modeled plaster figures of her performing *The Cobras* (fig. 3.7). He exaggerated the length of her arms to convey the snakes' sinuous pas de deux. Lachaise's expressive handling of plaster, rendering of rough surface texture, and emphasis on St. Denis's limbs echo Rodin's drawings of her. St. Denis's performances may have further influenced subsequent sculptures by Lachaise, as well as work by fellow Americans Paul Manship and Elie Nadelman, all of whom created modern sculpture grounded in classicism and the human form.[17]

The artists discussed thus far became interested in St. Denis because her undulating, pictorial choreography and exotic themes coincided with their

FIG. 3.6
Leo Rauth (German, 1884–1913), *Ruth St. Denis: Schlangentanz* (*Snake Dance*), 1910, pochoir, 38 × 38 in. (96.52 × 96.52 cm). Jacob's Pillow Dance Festival Archives; Donated by Tricia Henry Young.

own desire to break free of academic constraints in favor of a more personal and expressive style. However, in 1910, caricaturist Marius de Zayas published a less flattering image of St. Denis and her cobras in Alfred Stieglitz's journal *Camera Work* (fig. 3.8), which, like Stieglitz's 291 gallery, influenced the emergence of a self-consciously American avant-garde. In de Zayas's rendition, the elasticity of St. Denis's arms is played for humor rather than as innovative modern dance. De Zayas stripped the veil of spirituality and mystery that St. Denis attempted to instill in her work, instead presenting *The Cobras*—and St. Denis—as melodramatic and slightly ridiculous.[18]

Pictorial critique notwithstanding, St. Denis toured nonstop after she returned to the United States, finally earning enough money to produce *Egypta* in 1910 (fig. 3.9), a concert-length program that she originally conceived in 1904. The performance featured a large company of dancers and elaborate sets based on ancient Egyptian mythology and religious texts, including *The Book of the Dead*. *Egypta* suggested that St. Denis had greater ambitions than to remain a soloist mainly inspired by India, and indeed her next piece, *O-Mika* (see p. 28), was influenced by Japan.

In 1912, during an extended stay in Los Angeles, St. Denis connected with the city's Japanese community, where she took dance lessons from a former geisha and attended performances of traditional Noh theater.[19] Drawing on those experiences, *O-Mika* had several acts and included spoken-word interludes, creating a combination of theater and dance that St. Denis labeled "dance drama." Japanese performers taught St. Denis steps, a Japanese designer created the extensive sets, and St. Denis hired Japanese actors for the production, following the pattern established in *Radha* of using native labor to signal that her work was authentic. At St. Denis's request, one of the Japanese actors, Momotaro Toyama, spoke about the accuracy of the production, particularly the set design, to the *New-York Tribune*, which described him as a philologist who could not find work in the United States.[20]

FIG. 3.7
Gaston Lachaise (American, born France, 1882–1935), *Snake Dance, Ruth St. Denis*, 1910, plaster, 6¼ × 6 × 3 in. (15.9 × 15.2 × 7.6 cm). Metropolitan Museum of Art, New York; Bequest of Allys Lachaise, 1967, 68.91.5.

FIG. 3.8
Marius de Zayas (American, born Mexico, 1880–1961), *Ruth St. Denis, Camera Work 46*, 1910, photogravure, image: 8⅝ × 6⁷⁄₁₆ in. (21.9 × 16.3 cm); sheet: 8¹³⁄₁₆ × 6⁹⁄₁₆ in. (22.4 × 16.7 cm). Philadelphia Museum of Art; Gift of Carl Zigrosser, 1966-205-29(11).

FIG. 3.9
Sarony Studios, New York (American, 1898–1926), *Ruth St. Denis in Costume for Egypta*, 1910, photograph, 5⅞ × 3⅞ in. (14.9 × 9.8 cm). Jacob's Pillow Dance Festival Archives.

O-Mika continued St. Denis's exploration of the theme of transformation from human to divine and vice versa found in *Radha* and *Egypta*. She played a courtesan who performed a series of dances, including one based on Ikebana and a martial spear dance. A posed image by the Japanese American photographer Soichi Sunami shows St. Denis at the beginning of the dance, wearing multiple layers of kimonos (fig. 3.10). At the end of each of the dances in the performance, St. Denis threw off a kimono until, with a final flourish, she revealed herself to be the Bodhisattva Fugen-Bosatsu, associated with compassion in Japanese Buddhism.

St. Denis's costumes in *O-Mika*, particularly the heavy outer kimono and obi sash, are arguably as much an actor in the production as St. Denis, and these garments influenced her choreography.[21] Although reviews of the piece were mixed to poor, the costumes stunned. In his biography of St. Denis, Shawn quotes theater critic Charles Darnton describing "her Japanese costumes, robes gorgeous beyond description and so much a part of her that you readily conclude she must have dreamed them. The most matter-of-fact spectator would be willing to swear this darling of the gods could have nothing to do with a 'dressmaker.'"[22] In her 1914 vaudeville compendium (notably illustrated by de Zayas), Caroline Caffin wrote that St. Denis's appearance "had the boldly patterned refinement of the old Japanese prints, with their flowing lines and richly sombre coloring."[23]

O-Mika debuted in New York in March 1913, coinciding with the infamous International Exhibition of Modern Art, better known as the Armory Show. This exhibition introduced Modernist art to many Americans for the first time, causing much cultural controversy. At least one critic found that *O-Mika* had unpleasant similarities to the radical new work at the Armory Show. In an unsigned review titled "Miss St. Denis Puzzles in New Dancing Act," the critic wrote:

> After two and one-half hours at the Fulton Theatre last night one went away convinced that the futurists, who have laid violent hands on art, at last have extended their influence to the drama, and so far as the average citizen is concerned with results about unsatisfactory and unfathomable . . . one felt for sure the futurists of art had cast their spell over Miss St. Denis. They should be made to suffer for their sins.[24]

It seems puzzling now to compare St. Denis in *O-Mika* to a "futurist" painting like Duchamp's *Nude Descending a Staircase* (fig. 3.11), perhaps the most notorious work from the Armory Show. However, St. Denis's manipulation of

her costume during the performance may have led the critic to the analogy. Although the kimono from *O-Mika* in the Jacob's Pillow Dance Festival Archives is not St. Denis's first, Darnton's and Caffin's descriptions indicate that the original was likely as heavily embroidered and brightly colored as its later replacement. Moving across a stage in kimonos with complex decorative patterns of flora and fauna rendered in shimmering silk and metallic thread (fig. 3.12), highlighted by spotlights, and then suddenly dropping them at the close of a section, St. Denis would have been a dazzling sight, and perhaps resembled the fractured form of a moving body found in Duchamp's *Nude*.

Comparison between *O-Mika* and Modernist art also may have stemmed from St. Denis's subversion of her expected gender role as a passive object of sexual desire. The *O-Mika* costumes were more elaborate, and covered more of St. Denis's body, than her wardrobe in previous productions. This bothered the "puzzled" *Herald* critic as much as—if not more than—his purported inability to understand the story: "The lithe and sinuous Miss St. Denis usually pleases her audiences with some interesting interpretations. As barefoot and lightly clad dancers go she has long been recognized among the foremost."[25] Another critic, however, praised St. Denis's androgynous performance: "Here was no timidity or restraint but breezy, joyous exercise of boldness and muscle—woman's deftness and agility were matched with man's strength and skill, and that without fear or favor . . . this maiden will be able to take her own part, if physical bravery is ever demanded of her."[26]

FIG. 3.10
Soichi Sunami (American, born Japan, 1885–1971), *Ruth St. Denis in O-Mika*, not dated, photograph, 9¼ × 7 in. (23.5 × 17.8 cm). Jacob's Pillow Dance Festival Archives.

FIG. 3.11
Marcel Duchamp (American, born France, 1887–1968), *Nude Descending a Staircase (No. 2)*, 1912, oil on canvas, 57⅞ × 35⅛ in. (147 × 89.2 cm). Philadelphia Museum of Art; The Louise and Walter Arensberg Collection, 1950, 1950-134-59.

FIG. 3.12, FACING
Detail of kimono from *O-Mika* (see p. 28).

FIG. 3.13
Morton Livingston Schamberg (American, 1881–1918), *Study of a Girl (Fanette Reider)*, c. 1912, oil on canvas, 30 11/16 × 23 1/8 in. (78 × 58.8 cm). Williams College Museum of Art; Bequest of Lawrence H. Bloedel, Class of 1923, 77.9.11.

Instead of exposing her body, St. Denis covered it up and took on traditionally masculine traits. In the era of the "New Woman," of which St. Denis is a good example for carving out an independent career as a solo performer largely without relying on male patronage, her androgyny may well have particularly rankled critics. Modern artists' experimentation in rendering the human body with reductive, fragmented, or exaggerated features that obscured markers of gender could be found in other works of art at the Armory Show, including Morton Livingston Schamberg's *Study of a Girl (Fanette Reider)* (fig. 3.13). Regardless of whether others in the audience of *O-Mika* made explicit —unfavorable—comparisons between the dance drama and avant-garde art being shown nearby, *O-Mika* was a box office failure and closed early. In the common refrain of the avant-garde to negative criticism, Ted Shawn later characterized *O-Mika* as "the highest artistic achievement of the season; from the standpoint of popular response it failed," and he went on to note that the dance drama gained popularity later.[27] In Shawn's view, hoi polloi were not ready for *O-Mika* when it debuted in 1913, just as many were not ready for modern art.

Ruth St. Denis and Ted Shawn: The Denishawn Years

Although Ted Shawn had seen St. Denis perform in 1911, he did not meet her until 1914, when he auditioned to accompany her on a tour of the United States. In August, only a few months into their professional relationship, they married. Initially, their performances were still billed under St. Denis's name, but as Shawn achieved celebrity as the most famous American male dancer, they

FIG. 3.14
John Singer Sargent (American, 1856–1925), *Thomas Eugene McKeller* (formerly titled *Ted Shawn*), c. 1915, collotype, 20¾ × 17¾ in. (52.7 × 45.1 cm). National Portrait Gallery, Smithsonian Institution, S/NPG.84.181.

chose the portmanteau Denishawn for their company and school. As noted in the introduction to this essay, Denishawn became the first significant dance company in the United States—and the first deemed such an international box office draw that they were able to mount a successful tour of Asia.[28]

Unlike St. Denis, Shawn had not been a subject for artists during the early part of his career. However, the year after Shawn partnered with St. Denis, John Singer Sargent may have sketched him while the artist worked on murals for the Boston Public Library. Recently, curators at the Isabella Stewart Gardner Museum have argued that this likeness (fig. 3.14), long presumed to depict Shawn, is actually of Thomas McKeller, a Black elevator operator who became Sargent's favorite American model. Sargent whitewashed most images of McKeller, putting Caucasian heads on his Black body. St. Denis and Sargent had crossed paths in London, and they knew the same people in Boston's artistic circles, including Gardner. Because of these connections, it could be that Sargent did either sketch Shawn, or grafted his white head onto McKeller's body.[29]

St. Denis and Shawn had grand ambitions for Denishawn. The company became the training ground for the first generation of dancers in the United States considered truly Modernist, including Martha Graham, Doris Humphrey, and Charles Weidman. Shawn contributed pieces with Native American, ancient Greek, Aztec, and Spanish flamenco influences to St. Denis's mainly Asian repertoire. However, India continued to be a strong inspiration for St. Denis. In 1914, she debuted a new solo, *The Legend of the Peacock* (fig. 3.15),

FIG. 3.15
Ira L. Hill (American, 1877–1947), *Ruth St. Denis in Costume for The Legend of the Peacock*, 1914, photograph, 5 × 4 in. (12.7 × 10.2 cm). Jacob's Pillow Dance Festival Archives.

at Ravinia Park, an outdoor venue near Chicago. The dance, supposedly based on an Indian legend, finds St. Denis transformed from a human dancer into a peacock. Manipulating the long train of her costume (see p. 20), St. Denis strutted around the stage as a bird still clinging to a vestige of its former humanity.[30] *The Legend of the Peacock* became, like *Radha*, a signature of her career. The costume, although much altered, still gives a sense of how St. Denis would have looked on stage: almost every part of it is designed to reflect light, producing what must have been a powerful iridescent effect.

American painter Robert Henri asked St. Denis to sit for him wearing the peacock costume (see p. 21), believing that a portrait of her dressed for her popular solo would be good publicity for them both.[31] In the 1919 portrait, St. Denis stands in an exaggerated S-curve, suggesting her upper-body flexibility as well as the long lines of a peacock's throat, body, and train. Henri draws attention to St. Denis's exposed midriff and bare feet, starkly contrasting the paleness of her skin with the background. By highlighting her flesh, Henri deftly captured the boundary St. Denis navigated between creating serious dance and courting controversy with her revealing costumes. As with many artists' images of St. Denis and Shawn, Henri's painting, with its rich colors rendered in thick oleaginous paint, coupled with the extant costume, gives a much better sense of St. Denis's appearance on stage than black-and-white photography and film footage from the time can convey.

St. Denis was a natural subject for Henri. At the turn of the twentieth century, he led a group of artists called the Ashcan School, who depicted urban life—including dance, theater, and sporting events—in a gritty, realist style. The Ashcan School represented a modernizing force in American art, expanding the stylistic and representational options for American artists both through their coarse application of paint and in their images of urban poverty and provocative forms of entertainment, such as burlesque. Their work, like St. Denis's, was modern but not Modernist. For her part, St. Denis was pleased to associate herself with Henri, an artist who had long been characterized as being oppositional to the status quo.

FIG. 3.16
Edward Buk Ulreich (American, born Hungary, 1884–1966), *Ruth St. Denis in The Legend of the Peacock*, c. 1920, watercolor over pencil on paper-faced cardboard, 22½ × 24¼ in. (57.2 × 61.6 cm). Jacob's Pillow Dance Festival Archives.

By 1919, six years after the Armory Show, Henri and the Ashcan School seemed conservative. Although few Americans were creating true avant-garde work at the time of the exhibition in 1913, artists quickly began exploring the new means of rendering objects and bodies they had experienced there. Henri was one of several American artists who looked to contemporary dance for inspiration after the Armory Show. The abstracted and rhythmic movements of modern dancers provided a model for escaping convention—as St. Denis had—and suggested novel methods for depicting the body in motion.[32] St. Denis was also American, which may have evinced some nationalistic pride among artists like Henri—as well as Shawn—who found themselves in the shadow of European modern art.[33] In his portrait of St. Denis, Henri depicted a dancer associated—as he had been as a painter—with innovation; he also shared with her the challenge of representing a chimera, a woman dancing in the body of a male bird, but neither fully human nor fully animal.

For the first headquarters of Denishawn, St. Denis and Shawn rented a home in Los Angeles. Shawn commissioned Hungarian-born artist and designer Edward Buk Ulreich to create murals and furniture for the space.[34] Ulreich also painted St. Denis in her peacock costume (fig. 3.16). His watercolor places her in a stagelike space, with a column on the far left and a sprig

FIG. 3.17
Albert Herter (American, 1871–1950), *Ruth St. Denis in Costume for Kuan-Yin*, 1925, oil on canvas, 90 × 40 in. (228.6 × 101.6 cm). Jacob's Pillow Dance Festival Archives.

of vegetation at right. St. Denis's right arm is raised as she leans back slightly, capturing the hubris of the character.[35] Whereas Henri's St. Denis is solid and fleshy, even a little louche, Ulreich portrays her as thin and ethereal, employing an Art Nouveau aesthetic that extended into his furniture design and wall decoration.

A few years after Henri painted St. Denis, Albert Herter created monumental portraits of her (fig. 3.17) and Shawn (see fig. 3.1). His family had founded the Herter Brothers furniture and interior design firm in New York, which like Tiffany & Company is associated with the opulence of the Gilded Age. Herter had ambitions to become a painter, however, and trained in Paris. He is mostly known for his portraits, but he carried on his family interests in design, creating tapestries and murals. At his Santa Barbara estate, El Marisol, he also wrote and directed an epic Orientalist play, *The Gift of Eternal Life: An Indo-Persian Legend*, in which St. Denis performed the lead.

Herter portrayed St. Denis in costume for *Kuan-Yin*, a solo that she had created in 1919. It may be the dance for which St. Denis relied most on artwork she had viewed in museums.[36] At some point, she had a pedestal and mandorla made for her to stand within, reinforcing the connection between the dance and its sculptural origins (fig. 3.18). For the dance, St. Denis wore complicated body jewelry on her torso, waist, and legs, while a bejeweled crown sat upon her head (figs. 3.19–22). Gold lamé drapery descended the length of her body, pooling at her feet. The costume precluded any quick or complex movements—it would have been easy to get tangled up in the drapery and jewelry—so the dance consisted of St. Denis creating mudras, symbolic

FIG. 3.18
Soichi Sunami (American, born Japan, 1855–1971), *Ruth St. Denis in Costume for Kuan-Yin*, not dated, photograph, 10¼ × 8 in. (26 × 20.3 cm). Jacob's Pillow Dance Festival Archives.

FIG. 3.19
Costume worn by Ruth St. Denis for *Kuan-Yin*, 1919, glass, metal, feathers, ceramic beads, plastic, silk, and cotton (replica cloak and underskirt made in 2018). Ruth St. Denis UCLA Costume Collection, Jacob's Pillow Dance Festival Archives, C-022_a-c.

hand gestures used in Hindu and Buddhist ritual contexts and dance, as well as some slow and deliberate steps.

Herter captures the stillness of *Kuan-Yin*, depicting St. Denis enveloped in columnar drapery and holding a lotus flower, with prayer beads, the bejeweled crown, and a hint of the body jewelry visible. St. Denis stands on a pedestal shaped like a lotus, and she is inscribed within a golden mandorla. While Henri emphasized that St. Denis was made of flesh and bone, Herter transformed her into the ethereal, supernatural being that she sought to convey in the performance.[37]

Photography of St. Denis in her *Kuan-Yin* costume captures the tension between spirit and skin. Former Denishawn dancer and dance historian Jane Sherman wrote that St. Denis had two costumes for this work. The first is represented in Herter's portrait and photographs by Soichi Sunami. The

FIG. 3.20
Detail of headdress for *Kuan-Yin* showing a central flower decorated with kingfisher feathers (tian-tsui), C-022_a.

FIG. 3.21
Detail of body jewelry, costume for *Kuan-Yin*, C-022_c.

FIG. 3.22
Detail of beads, costume for *Kuan-Yin*, C-022_c.

FIG. 3.23
Nickolas Muray (American, born Hungary, 1892–1965), *Ruth St. Denis in Costume for Kuan-Yin*, c. 1921, photograph, 10 × 8 in. (25.4 × 20.3 cm). Jacob's Pillow Dance Festival Archives.

second costume, seen in a photograph by Hungarian-born fashion photographer Nickolas Muray (fig. 3.23), did away with the enveloping drapery, instead leaving her torso looking as though covered only in a thin sash and jewelry.[38] Muray also posed St. Denis with her arms lifted over her head and looking slightly downward, calling attention to her apparently nude chest and stomach.

Although *Kuan-Yin* marked an even more spiritual turn in St. Denis's choreography, it was not an audience pleaser. Shawn dissuaded St. Denis from opening Denishawn tour dates with it in favor of more lively numbers. For St. Denis's second solo as the character Kuan-Yin, 1926's *White Jade*, she incorporated aspects of Chinese art that she had encountered on the Denishawn tour of Asia into a similarly sculptural dance. Ziegfeld Follies management cut *White Jade* from the Denishawn American tour in 1927 because of poor audience reaction.[39] As a publicity image, Muray's *Kuan-Yin* photograph suggested drama in a dance that had little of it.

In the pendant to his *Kuan-Yin* portrait of St. Denis, Herter depicted Shawn in costume for *The Feather of the Dawn* (see fig. 3.1). He posed the feather-clad Shawn on demi-pointe standing at the edge of a precipice in the American Southwest, as though about to leap from his perch to soar among mountains

FIG. 3.24
Margaret Evans Price (American, 1888–1973), *The Feather of the Dawn*, not dated, colored pencil on board, 14 × 19½ in. (35.56 × 49.5 cm). Jacob's Pillow Dance Festival Archives.

and mesas—as Shawn is depicted doing in a drawing by illustrator Margaret Evans Price (fig. 3.24). In the 1920s, Shawn had increasingly become a cultural nationalist, an ideology he would imbue into his choreography for the Men Dancers. In his pursuit of uniquely American art, he joined other American artists, writers, and choreographers who looked for inspiration at home, in Anglo-American folk traditions and Indigenous American cultures, instead of in Europe.[40] *The Feather of the Dawn*, which premiered in 1923, is the ultimate example of his making ersatz versions of Native American rituals despite their objections, as discussed in the beginning of this essay.

The two portraits hung at the Denishawn studios, visually reinforcing the pair as matriarch and patriarch of the company and school.[41] The school was critical to their idea of dance as an integrated humanistic art form (fig. 3.25). Students took classes in a variety of dance styles, but they also studied theory and literature selected to edify and strengthen their minds and learned costume making and set design. In 1917, St. Denis wrote in *Vogue* that their eventual goal was to establish "the greater 'Denishawn,' where, we dream, painters, musicians, poets, and authors shall come to bide a while and give and gain inspiration."[42] Shawn echoed this sentiment years later: "Denishawn in its ultimate development into an ideal institution is first and foremost that it be a place where life is lived as an art."[43]

Despite their modern leanings, Shawn and St. Denis's emphasis on the bodies, minds, and spirits of their students, as well as their combination of the performing and visual arts, demonstrates their affinity with the Arts and Crafts movement, which began in the United Kingdom during the mid-nineteenth century but soon found footholds in the United States. Adherents valorized handcrafting as a rejection of the dehumanizing labor of industrial factories and the unhealthy pace of life engendered by modern technology.[44] Both St. Denis and Shawn had experienced the social reformist ideas that accompanied the Arts and Crafts movement and were skeptical of some aspects of modern life, which led, in part, to their appropriation of "traditional" cultures. They believed more authentic expressions of self and

FIG. 3.25
Putnam and Valentine, Los Angeles (c. 1880–1930), *Students in Studio at Denishawn School, Los Angeles*, 1917, photograph, 8 × 10 in. (20.3 × 25.4 cm). Jacob's Pillow Dance Festival Archives.

of spirit lay in cultures they considered less affected by the speed of life in the United States and Europe. Shawn contrasted modern decadence with the healthy values he perceived in Native American and other cultures in his book *The American Ballet.*[45] For her part, St. Denis associated with people who provided intellectual leadership to Arts and Crafts–influenced anti-Modernism in the United States, many of whom were also exploring Asian religions and cultural practices, including historian of Japanese art Ernest Fenollosa, who saw St. Denis perform *Radha* early in her career.[46]

St. Denis and Shawn commissioned the Roycroft Press to produce the *Denishawn Magazine* (fig. 3.26). After meeting William Morris, one of the leading lights of the Arts and Crafts movement, Elbert Hubbard had founded the Roycroft commune in East Aurora, New York, to create artisanal furniture and household goods within a guild-like labor structure. In time, Roycroft became most noted for its books and other printed materials.[47] The communal way of life and work at Roycroft impressed Shawn, who announced that he wanted to create a similar guild for dancers under the Denishawn name, hoping to provide better labor protections for performers.

Denishawn Magazine, the first issue of which sold twenty thousand copies, was heavily illustrated with drawings and photographs.[48] Rose O'Neill and

Bernice Oehler designed many of the decorative page borders, the line drawings of Shawn and St. Denis, and the Denishawn logo of intertwined androgynous embryonic humanoid forms.[49] Their styles, much like that of Denishawn itself, looked to history for inspiration, including Egyptian hieroglyphics, medieval illuminated manuscripts, and the neoclassical drawings of British artist John Flaxman. The designers created Art Deco–inflected branding for Denishawn that looked backward rather than to contemporary Modernist art (fig. 3.27). Denishawn incorporated O'Neill's and Oehler's images into other promotional materials, including brochures for the school and performance announcements.

The zenith of Denishawn was during its tour of East and South Asia from 1925 to 1927 (see figs. 4.3 and 4.10). The company took frequent lessons from local practitioners, and St. Denis was finally able to see the kind of Indian dance she had been creating pastiches of for twenty years. She and Shawn also studied Japanese dance from masters at the Imperial Theatre in Tokyo, where Denishawn had two lengthy residencies. The Imperial Theatre workshops made costumes and props for the company. Denishawn also acquired textiles and jewelry throughout its travels for use in future costumes, which added superficial accuracy to the troupe's choreography.

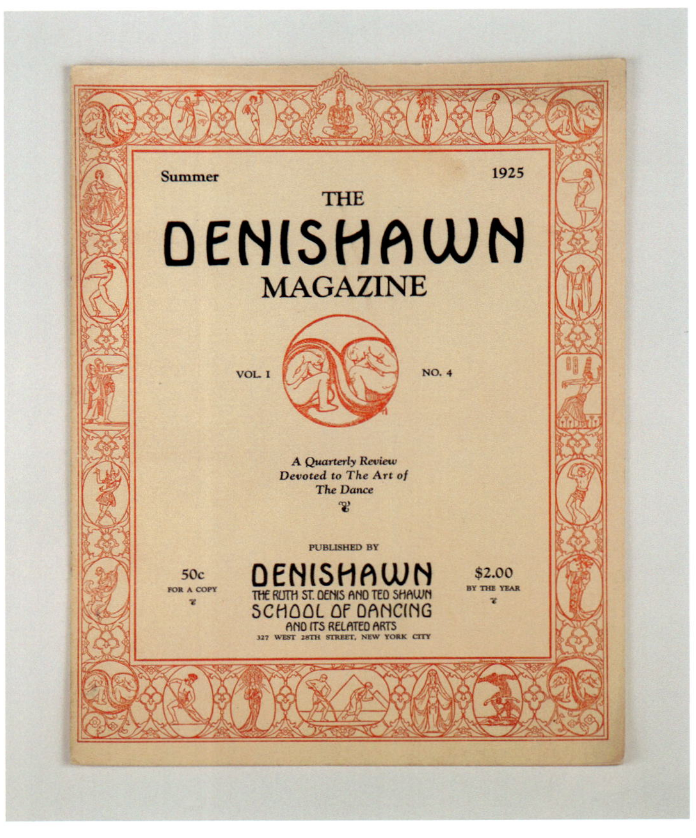
Summer 1925
THE
DENISHAWN
MAGAZINE
VOL. I NO. 4
A Quarterly Review
Devoted to The Art of
The Dance
PUBLISHED BY
50c FOR A COPY
DENISHAWN
THE RUTH ST. DENIS AND TED SHAWN
SCHOOL OF DANCING
AND ITS RELATED ARTS
327 WEST 28TH STREET, NEW YORK CITY
$2.00 BY THE YEAR

FIG. 3.26
Roycroft Press, *The Denishawn Magazine* 1, no. 4 (Summer 1925). Jacob's Pillow Dance Festival Archives.

FIG. 3.27, FACING
Bernice Oehler (American, 1881–1955), illustration in Denishawn souvenir program, 1923. Jacob's Pillow Dance Festival Archives.

The largest prop Denishawn commissioned in South Asia was the set for Shawn's *Cosmic Dance of Siva* (fig. 3.28). Likely made in Calcutta (now Kolkata), it consists of a shallow stage with a front piece carved in bas-relief featuring dancing figures, animals, and demons. This piece slides into grooves set into two wooden colonnettes, which contain lights covered by red gels that bathed Shawn in a fiery glow. Surmounting the stage is a pedestal decorated like a lotus flower, on which rests a demonic figure that Shawn, as Shiva in the guise of cosmic dancer Nataraja, would vanquish, framed by a circular wooden mandorla with inset cast-iron flames. The entire structure is designed to erect and break down quickly and easily, with all the pieces fitting into crates that doubled as the stage. During performances, Shawn would beat a percussive instrument made of two human skullcaps. He also lit powdered incense placed at the front of the platform, heightening the drama as smoke reflected the red stage lighting, and incorporating aural and olfactory components (fig. 3.29).

After Denishawn returned from Asia, Shawn and St. Denis built a large Moorish-style studio, residence, and school in the Bronx, scaling up Shawn's idea of a school of arts modeled on the Roycroft commune.[50] Denishawn also pursued a relentless performance schedule at venues throughout the United

RUTH ST DENIS
TED SHAWN
DANCE OF
THE REBIRTH
©
Bernice Oehler

FIG. 3.28, FACING
Makers not identified (Kolkata, India), *Set for Cosmic Dance of Siva*, 1926, wood and metal, approximately 96 in. (243 cm) diameter, plus base. Jacob's Pillow Dance Festival Archives.

FIG. 3.29
Photographer not identified, *Ted Shawn in Cosmic Dance of Siva during Ziegfield Follies Tour*, 1928, photograph, overall 7⁵⁄₁₆ × 7⁵⁄₁₆ in. (18.6 × 18.6 cm). Jacob's Pillow Dance Festival Archives.

States, trying to keep afloat at the beginning of the Great Depression.[51] As the Depression affected the Denishawn enterprise, St. Denis and Shawn's personal relationship also frayed. The pair spent more and more time apart, with Shawn touring Europe in 1930 and 1931. Their marriage had never been traditionally monogamous or heteronormative, and they amicably agreed to separate in 1930 but never legally divorced. Shawn's subsequent amorous relationships were with men, including a long partnership with Barton Mumaw, who was a principal member of the Men Dancers.[52] Denishawn officially ended in 1931.

After Denishawn: Ted Shawn's Late Career

As St. Denis and Shawn struggled with their relationship at the beginning of the Great Depression in the United States, Shawn attracted the patronage of Katherine Dreier. She, along with artists Marcel Duchamp and Man Ray, founded the Société Anonyme, Inc., in 1920 to foster the appreciation of modern art in the United States. The group collected and exhibited work by Wassily Kandinsky, Piet Mondrian, Constantin Brancusi, Arthur Dove, and Paul Klee, among many others.

Today, Shawn is not often identified with the formal Modernism championed by the Société Anonyme, and he explicitly declined to associate with European Modernists on tours of Germany in 1930 and 1931 funded by the Société. Dreier introduced Shawn to artists and dancers, hoping to convert him to Modernism. However, Shawn dismissed what he saw as innovation for innovation's sake, and he found much abstract choreography ugly. He did make at least one exception, doing some nude modeling for German sculptor Georg Kolbe (fig. 3.30).[53] Back in the United States, Shawn also complained about modern social dances such as the Charleston and the Lindy Hop, partially on racist terms because of their origin in African American dance.[54] As late as 1936, in the epic piece *O, Libertad!*, the Men Dancers wore identical disconcerting and feminized masks as they imitated jazz dancing to convey the decadence of the 1920s (see p. 100).

FIG. 3.30
Georg Kolbe (German, 1877–1947), *Study of Ted Shawn*, 1930, ink on paper, 18½ × 14 in. (47 × 35.6 cm). Jacob's Pillow Dance Festival Archives.

Although Shawn brushed off Dreier's attempts to persuade him to embrace Modernism, the two held similar beliefs about the progress of human enlightenment, and the importance of kinesthetic movement to it, which were partially grounded in their cultural nationalist reading of Theosophy.[55] Her images were influenced by Theosophical ideas of human evolution, and Shawn eventually created a piece for the Men Dancers after a 1934 suite of forty abstract prints by Dreier (fig. 3.31). Shawn's piece, *A Dreier Lithograph*, features the dancers interpreting the shapes and directionality suggested by lines and arrows in her composition.

Earlier in their friendship, Dreier had painted a dynamic portrait of Shawn, *Abstract Psychological Portrait of Ted Shawn* (fig. 3.32). Although the title of the 1929 portrait suggests it reveals Shawn's inner state of mind, the forms in

FIG. 3.31
Katherine Sophie Dreier (American, 1877–1952), *Forty Variations*, published 1937, lithograph with hand coloring and pochoir, 8½ × 11⅞ in. (21.59 × 30.16 cm). Harvard Art Museums / Fogg Museum; Gift of Theodore Dreier and Barbara B. Dreier on behalf of Katherine S. Dreier bequest, 2007.202.6.

FIG. 3.32
Katherine Sophie Dreier (American, 1877–1952), *The Psychological Abstract Portrait of Ted Shawn*, 1929, oil on canvas, 32 × 25 in. (81.28 × 63.5 cm). Munson-Williams-Proctor Arts Institute; Purchased in honor of the Museum's current and former docents, 96.29.

the painting, including the triangle on the right and concentric swirling circles that occupy much of the canvas, instead anticipate the energetic and muscular choreography Shawn would create for himself as a soloist after parting with St. Denis the following year, and that he would continue to produce for the Men Dancers.[56]

In 1931, at the height of his working relationship with Dreier, Shawn bought a dilapidated farm in Becket, Massachusetts, on ancestral homelands of the

FIG. 3.33,
Shapiro Studios, Pittsfield, Massachusetts (American, c. 1929–1976), *Ted Shawn and Men Dancers in Costume for Earth from Dance of the Ages*, 1938, photograph, 8 × 10 in. (20.3 × 25.4 cm). Jacob's Pillow Dance Festival Archives.

Agawam, the Nipmuc, the Pocumtuc, and the Mohican. In one of countless actions erasing Indigenous histories of New England, white colonists had named the farm Jacob's Pillow because a large, pillow-shaped stone on the property reminded them of a rock in an Old Testament story. In Massachusetts, Shawn increasingly began to choreograph for men, and by 1933 had gathered a small group of male dancers who then became his Men Dancers company. At Jacob's Pillow, Shawn realized the goals of establishing an idyllic homosocial commune of artists who worked, lived, learned, and created together. The Men Dancers lasted until 1940, when many of the men enlisted in the army.

During its seven-year run, Ted Shawn and His Men Dancers toured the country frequently, performing anywhere they could to make a case for the importance of men in dance. Their pieces included partnering in pas de deux and large-group performances, where the often scantily clad dancers were in close contact, queering American dance. There does not seem to have been much collaboration between American or European visual artists and the company, aside from dramatic photographs of the men, set against the backdrop of the Berkshire hills, produced by a local studio (fig. 3.33). Interestingly, though, Shawn chose abstract, recognizably Modernist images for promotional materials for the Men Dancers, such as covers for programs by the European émigrés and graphic artists Werner Drewes and Constantin Alajálov (figs. 3.34 and 3.35), perhaps to signal the radical nature of his all-male enterprise.

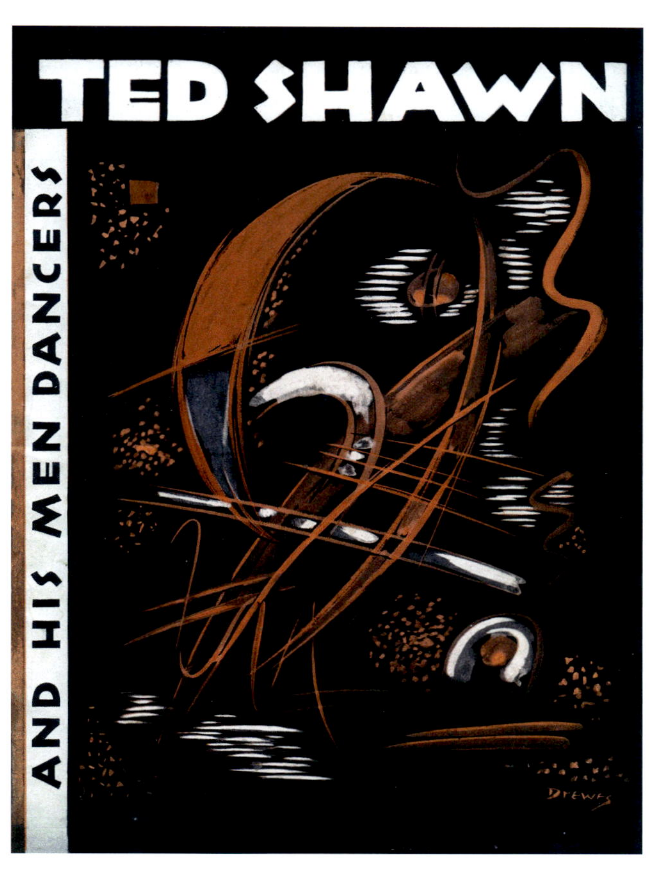

FIG. 3.34
Werner Drewes (American, born Germany, 1899–1985), *Ted Shawn and His Men Dancers Souvenir Program*, 1936, 11⁹⁄₁₆ × 8³⁄₈ in. (29.4 × 21.3 cm). Jacob's Pillow Dance Festival Archives.

FIG. 3.35
Constantin Alajálov (American, born Russia, 1900–1987), *Ted Shawn and His Men Dancers Souvenir Program*, c. 1934, 11½ × 8³⁄₈ in. (29.2 × 21.3 cm). Jacob's Pillow Dance Festival Archives.

FIG. 3.36, FACING
Major Felten (American, 1904–1975), *Ted Shawn in Fire from Dance of the Ages*, c. 1938, oil on canvas, 32 × 28 in. (81.3 × 71.1 cm). Jacob's Pillow Dance Festival Archives.

Shawn also commissioned artist and illustrator Major Felten to create dramatic promotional materials for the Men Dancers, including a poster in the style of Rockwell Kent's wood engravings. Felten also depicted Shawn in costume for the "Fire" section of *Dance of the Ages*, which is probably Shawn's best-known work today. The dance tackles themes of the history and future of humanity through four movements symbolic of fire, water, earth, and air. In each of the acts, Shawn portrays a different kind of leader: shaman (fire), poet-philosopher (water), demagogue (earth), and finally the leader of a post-apocalyptic utopia (air).[57]

The opening movement, "Fire," is perhaps the most dramatic, especially in terms of its costumes—black, hooded capes that are flung open to reveal bright red interior fabric, with the dancers otherwise clad only in high-cut, flesh-colored briefs. Felten portrays Shawn as the shaman (fig. 3.36). Standing on a raised stage, he leans back slightly, placing his body on a left-to-right diagonal. Shawn's arms are in an angular and exaggerated position as though he is about to lash out violently or perhaps throw a weapon. His legs are in demi-plié, which helps imply movement and assists in making Shawn take up more of the canvas. Seemingly standing within arcs of red flame, Shawn appears as a powerful leader commanding younger men—the role he played as leader of the Men Dancers.

Conclusion

Ruth St. Denis and Ted Shawn, both separately and together, utilized visual imagery in their dance compositions and as a critical component of their (often highly successful) promotional strategies. They partnered with American and European artists working in a variety of styles to help shape their images first as soloists, then for Denishawn, and finally, for Ted Shawn and His Men Dancers. Visual material publicizing Denishawn and its stars usually featured dancers costumed in textiles sourced from around the world—along with "authentic" accessories assembled from costume jewelry—reinforcing the Orientalist and colonial ideologies that informed their works. Imagery, costumes, choreography, and even makeup combined to portray St. Denis's and Shawn's white bodies as Other, appealing to their audiences' taste for the "exotic." They did so without acknowledging (or even recognizing) that they were profiting off of the cultural labor of bodies of color, whether in the form of dance lessons St. Denis received from Indian immigrants, decontextualized narrative and costume elements, or Shawn's appropriation of Hopi dance.

It is perhaps fitting that ballet impresario Lincoln Kirstein commissioned collage and assemblage artist Joseph Cornell to create the cover of the 1942 issue of *Dance Index* magazine devoted to the "Denishawn Era" (fig. 3.37). Cornell, like Denishawn, seemed both in and out of his time, making handcrafted boxes filled with found objects often representing the past, and pregnant with esoteric meaning. Cornell idolized

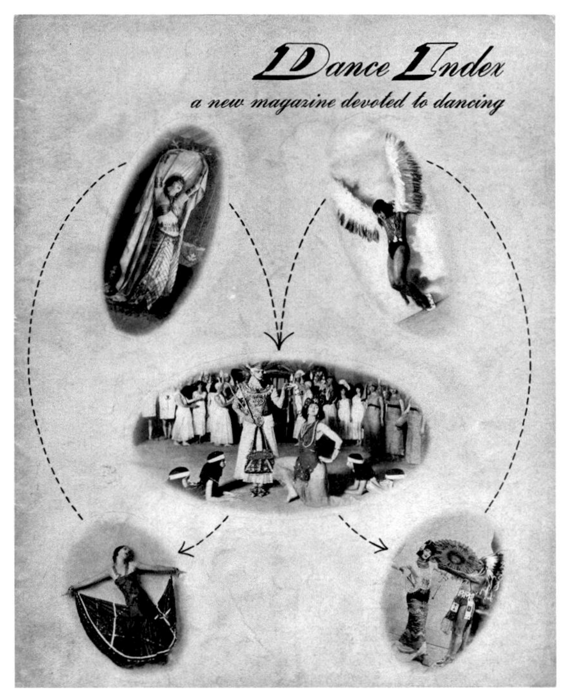

FIG. 3.37
Joseph Cornell (American, 1903–1972), cover of *Dance Index* 1, no. 6 (1942). Collection of Patsy Gay.

ballerinas from Romantic-era ballets and the present, including members of the company that eventually became the New York City Ballet, which Kirstein founded with George Balanchine.[58] Cornell's work in collage and his boxes usually present a cavalcade of images and materials that provide a visual and sometimes haptic experience. In comparison, his Denishawn cover is sparsely populated, as though Cornell had trouble reconciling the full legacies of St. Denis, Shawn, and the company they created together. Instead, he made a structural diagram of St. Denis and Shawn in solos with dotted lines leading to the center, where Denishawn appears in the *Egyptian Ballet*. More dotted lines extend to the lower register where Martha Graham, Doris Humphrey, and Charles Weidman—the most famous of the modern dancers who emerged from Denishawn—appear. Cornell created the collage with images of the dancers in costumes representing the Denishawn repertoire. Shawn and Weidman are wearing costumes from *The Feather of the Dawn*; St. Denis appears in *The Vision of Aissoua*, which was based on dance Shawn had seen in North Africa; Graham in the "Moorish-Spanish" *Serenata Morisca*; Humphrey in *A Burmese Yen Pwe*, a recreation of *pwe* dances St. Denis and Humphrey saw in Burma (now Myanmar); and the Denishawn company in the aforementioned ancient Egyptian–inspired spectacle.[59] Outside of the five images of the dancers, dotted lines in a parenthesis-like shape enclose everyone, as though either reinforcing modern dance's debt to St. Denis and Shawn or, alternately, relegating the entire group to a closed system where everyone failed to escape from the cultural appropriation of Denishawn. Although perhaps the least interesting cover Cornell did for *Dance Index*, the image is suggestive of an ongoing reckoning with the complex legacies of Ruth St. Denis and Ted Shawn.

Notes

1. Suzanne Shelton, *Divine Dancer: The Biography of Ruth St. Denis* (Garden City, NY: Doubleday, 1981), 46.

2. Ruth St. Denis, interview with Walter Terry, 1960, Jerome Robbins Dance Division, New York Public Library, quoted in Shelton, *Divine Dancer*, 147.

3. See, for example, Clare Fitzgerald, *Hymn to Apollo: The Ancient World and the Ballets Russes* (New York: Institute for the Study of the Ancient World, New York University, 2019); Jane Pritchard et al., *Diaghilev and the Golden Age of the Ballets Russes, 1909–1929* (London: Victoria and Albert Museum, 2010); John E. Bowlt et al., *A Feast of Wonders: Sergei Diaghilev and the Ballets Russes* (New York: Rizzoli, 2009); and Alexander Schouvaloff, *The Art of the Ballets Russes: The Serge Lifar Collection of Theater Designs, Costumes, and Paintings* (Hartford, CT: Wadsworth Atheneum, 1997).

4. Priya Srinivasan, *Sweating Saris: Indian Dance as Transnational Labor* (Philadelphia: Temple University Press, 2011), 91.

5. Ted Shawn, *The American Ballet* (New York: Henry Holt, 1926), 15–20. For an overview of the several dances Shawn created on Indigenous American themes, see Jane Sherman, "The American Indian Imagery of Ted Shawn," *Dance Chronicle* 12, no. 3 (1989): 366–82.

6. Jesse Walter Fewkes, *Hopi Katcinas Drawn by Native Artists, Extract from the Twenty-First Annual Report of the Bureau of American Ethnology* (Washington, DC: Government Printing Office, 1904). For a full description of *The Feather of the Dawn*, see Jane Sherman, *The Drama of Denishawn Dance* (Middletown, CT: Wesleyan University Press, 1979), 90–94.

7. Jacqueline Shea Murphy, *The People Have Never Stopped Dancing: Native American Dance Histories* (Minneapolis: University of Minnesota Press, 2007), 84.

8. Shawn, *American Ballet*, 16.

9. Paul A. Scolieri, *Ted Shawn, His Life, Writings, and Dances* (New York: Oxford University Press, 2020), 24.

10. See Jane Desmond, "Dancing out the Difference: Cultural Imperialism and Ruth St. Denis's 'Radha' of 1906," *Signs* 17, no. 1 (Autumn, 1991): 28–49; Sherman, "American Indian Imagery of Ted Shawn"; and Edward Ross Dickinson, *Dancing in the Blood: Modern Dance and European Culture on the Eve of the First World War* (Cambridge: Cambridge University Press, 2017), 146–50.

11. Shelton, *Divine Dancer*, 26–49.

12. Bailey Van Hook, "The Early Career of Violet Oakley, Illustrator," *Women's Art Journal* 30, no. 1 (Spring/Summer, 2009): 29–38.

13. Desmond, "Dancing out the Difference," 32–33.

14. Ted Shawn lists the wives of American artists Karl Bitter, Edwin Blashfield, Arthur B. Davies, Orlando Rouland, and J. Alden Weir as sponsors of the first theater performance of *Radha*; Ted Shawn, *Pioneer and Prophet* (San Francisco: John Henry Nash, 1920), 1:10.

15. Juliet Bellow, "Beyond Movement: Auguste Rodin and the Dancers of His Time," in *Rodin and Dance: The Essence of Movement*, ed. Alexandra Gerstein (London: Courtauld Institute, 2016), 43; and Juliet Bellow and Nell Andrew, "Inventing Abstraction? Modernist Dance in Europe," in *The Modernist World*, ed. Stephen Ross and Allana Lindgren (London: Routledge, 2015), 330–32.

16. Bellow, "Beyond Movement," 45, 49.

17. The Smithsonian American Art Museum's Inventory of American Painting and Sculpture lists another sculpture by Lachaise of St. Denis in one of her Indian-inspired dances (Gaston Lachaise, *Ruth St. Denis—Veil Dance*, 1911, plaster, 9⅜ × 6½ × 4⅝ in.; http://siris-artinventories.si.edu/, control number: IAS 36240260). At the time of the inventory, it was listed as in the collection of the Museum of Modern Art in New York (acc. no. 1302.68), although it does not appear in the institution's online collection database today. St. Denis's dances may have also inspired the pose in a version of Lachaise's monumental *Standing Woman*, although the figure itself is based on the artist's wife, Isabel (Gaston Lachaise, *Elevation*, modeled 1912–15, cast 1930, cast bronze, 68 × 28 × 16 in.; Virginia Museum of Fine Arts, 78.8). JoLee Gillespie Stephens, "Modern Art and Modern Movement: Images of Dance in American Art, c. 1900–1950" (PhD diss., University of Kansas, 2011), 96–100. Stephens further argues that St. Denis's dancing influenced several sculptures by Paul Manship and Elie Nadelman. See also Susan Rather, *Archaism, Modernism, and the Art of Paul Manship* (Austin: University of Texas Press, 1993), 130.

18. Stephens, *Modern Art and Modern Movement*, 97.

19. Shawn, *Pioneer and Prophet*, 1:17; and Shelton, *Divine Dancer*, 103–4.

20. "Storiettes Heard Off Stage: Mr. Toyama Turns Actor, and Others Do Turns—Ruth St. Denis as a Japanese Dancer," *New-York Tribune*, March 9, 1913.

21. Shelton, *Divine Dancer*, 109. For other examples of costume affecting the choreography of St. Denis and Shawn, see Caroline Hamilton's essay in this volume, "'Fundamental Lines of Truth and Beauty': The Costumes of Ruth St. Denis, Denishawn, and Ted Shawn and His Men Dancers," pp. 35–45.

22. Shawn, *Pioneer and Prophet*, 58.

23. Caroline Caffin, with illustrations by Marius de Zayas, *Vaudeville* (New York: Mitchell Kennerley, 1914), 99.

24. "Miss St. Denis Puzzles in New Dancing Act," *New York Herald*, March 12, 1913. Paul Scolieri found a review of a Denishawn performance in Indiana from September of the following year, in which St. Denis's solos were also called "bizarre" and compared to Cubist art; Scolieri, *Ted Shawn, His Life*, 78.

25. "Miss St. Denis Puzzles."

26. Caffin, *Vaudeville*, 100. Caffin is specifically discussing the Spear Dance in *O-Mika*.

27. Shawn, *Pioneer and Prophet*, 59.

28. On St. Denis's and Shawn's deeply complicated relationships with each other and with the media during the founding of Denishawn and the announcement of their marriage, see accounts by their respective biographers: Shelton, *Divine Dancer*, 119–26; and Scolieri, *Ted Shawn, His Life*, 76–91.

29. Exhibition labels in *Boston's Apollo: Thomas McKeller and John Singer Sargent*, Isabella Stewart Gardner Museum, Boston, 2020. The Gardner titles the image *Study of a Seated Male Nude in a Roundel for the Rotunda of the Museum of Fine Arts, Boston*, http://www.gardnermuseum.org/sites/default/files/uploads/files/bostonsapollolabels_forweb_v2.pdf. The National Portrait Gallery in Washington, DC, formerly listed *Ted Shawn* as the title of its impression of the print but now indicates that McKeller is the subject, http://npg.si.edu/object/npg_S_NPG.84.181. The NPG also currently misattributes the subject of a photograph in their collection as ("possibly," according to the online catalogue entry) Ted Shawn, which Norton Owen brought to my attention; see Edwin F. Townsend, *Ted Shawn*, c. 1925, solarized gelatin silver print, 9 × 7⅜ in., NPG.81.10.

30. For a full description of the story and St. Denis's choreography, see Jane Sherman, *The Drama of Denishawn Dance* (Middletown, CT: Wesleyan University Press, 1979), 18–19.

31. Jane Dini, "Invitation to the Dance," in *Dance: American Art, 1830–1960*, ed. Jane Dini (Detroit: Detroit Institute of Art, 2016), 21.

32. Bruce Robertson, "American Modernism and Dance: Arthur B. Davies's *Dances*, 1915," in Dini, *Dance: American Art*, 115–33.

33. Shawn seemed to have felt himself to be in similar competition with the Ballets Russes, which he disparaged in his writing; Shawn, *American Ballet*, 11, 15.

34. Scolieri, *Ted Shawn, His Life*, 124. A table and one of the benches created by Ulreich is now in the collections of the Jacob's Pillow Dance Festival Archives, retaining much of its original paint.

35. Ulreich may have copied St. Denis's pose in the watercolor from a photograph by fashion and theater photographer Ira Hill.

36. Sherman, "Drama of Denishawn Dance," 45. Shawn characterized it as an "exquisite representation of Chinese porcelain"; Shawn, *Pioneer and Prophet*, 66–67.

37. See, for example, descriptions of Denishawn performing in New York City in 1924 and 1925: "Ruth St. Denis Returns," *New York Times*, April 4, 1924; and "Picturesque Dances by Ruth St. Denis," *New York Times*, March 18, 1925.

38. Sherman, *Drama of Denishawn Dance*, 45–46. St. Denis would have worn a body suit matching her skin, so there was no actual nudity.

39. Shelton, *Divine Dancer*, 160, 179. Sherman, *Drama of Denishawn Dance*, 156–57.

40. See for example, Wanda Corn, "Spiritual America" and "The Great American Thing," in *The Great American Thing: Modern Art and National Identity, 1915–1935* (Berkeley: University of California Press, 1999), 3–40, 239–91.

41. Until recently the portraits served the same function at Jacob's Pillow, hanging on either side of the proscenium in the Ted Shawn Theatre. They were removed for the *Dance We Must* exhibition at the Williams College

Museum of Art in 2018 and conserved at the Williamstown Art Conservation Center. Timothy Cahill chronicled the conservation process in "Dance They Must: New Life for Two Icons of Modern Dance," *Art Conservator* 13, no. 1 (February 18, 2019): 4–7, 14. After the exhibition, the original portraits were moved to the reading room of the Jacob's Pillow Dance Festival Archives, and full-scale facsimiles now hang in their place in the theater.

42. Ruth St. Denis, "The Education of the Dancer," *Vogue*, April 1, 1917, 136.

43. Shawn, *American Ballet*, 112.

44. On the development of the Arts and Crafts movement in the United States, and its connections to cultural elites, see T. J. Jackson Lears, *No Place of Grace: Antimodernism and the Transformation of American Culture, 1880–1920* (Chicago: University of Chicago Press, 1981), 66–83.

45. Shawn, *American Ballet*, 10.

46. Shelton, *Divine Dancer*, 58.

47. Lears, *No Place of Grace*, 68, 318–19.

48. Scolieri, *Ted Shawn, His Life*, 185, 187.

49. Shelton, *Divine Dancer*, 182.

50. Scolieri, *Ted Shawn, His Life*, 188, 225.

51. Shelton, *Divine Dancer*, 228–29.

52. Scolieri has written extensively about Shawn's homosexuality and his struggles in deciding how openly he could live as a gay man. Scolieri also discusses the consequences that implicit or explicit homophobia in earlier literature has had on Shawn's legacy; Scolieri, *Ted Shawn, His Life*, 2–4, 15–23, and 436–38.

53. Scolieri, *Ted Shawn, His Life*, 262–69.

54. Shawn, *American Ballet*, 7–8, 22. See also Robin Veder, *The Living Line: Modern Art and the Economy of Energy* (Hanover, NH: Dartmouth College Press, 2015), 255–56.

55. Veder, *Living Line*, 231–85.

56. Veder, *Living Line*, 276–78. Veder believes that the forms are also related to Theosophy.

57. Scolieri, *Ted Shawn, His Life*, 345–48.

58. See Elizabeth Welch, "From the Slipper of a Sylphide: A Box by Joseph Cornell," *Panorama* 4, no. 1 (Spring 2018), http://doi.org/10.24926/24716839.1640.

59. Descriptions of these dances are from Sherman, *Drama of Denishawn Dance*, 22–23, 119–21, and 142–43.

Kinetic Molpai, 1935

COMPANY
Ted Shawn and His Men Dancers

CHOREOGRAPHER
Ted Shawn

COMPOSER
Jess Meeker

Trousers worn by Fred Hearn and Barton Mumaw in *Kinetic Molpai*, 1935–38

Cotton, metal fastenings

Ted Shawn Costume Collection, Jacob's Pillow Dance Festival Archives, C-180_5, 7

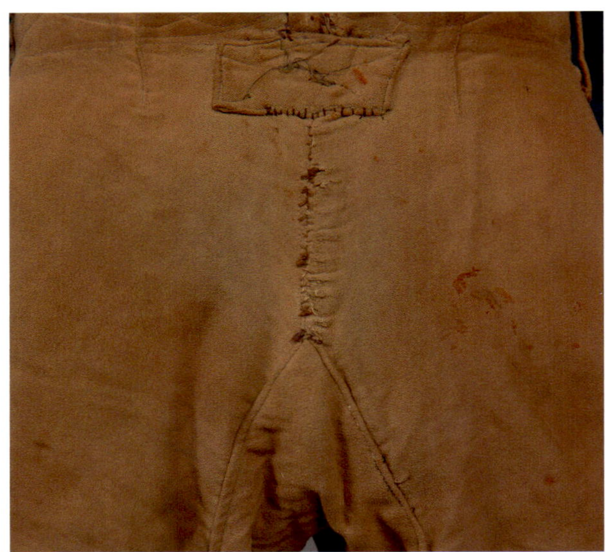

Detail from back of Barton Mumaw's costume showing multiple repairs and patches, C-180_7.

Shapiro Studios, Pittsfield, Massachusetts (American, c. 1929–1976), *Ted Shawn and His Men Dancers*, c. 1935, photograph, 7⅞ × 9⅞ in. (20 × 25.1 cm). Jacob's Pillow Dance Festival Archives.

These high-waisted trousers with wide-flared bottoms were made for the abstract work *Kinetic Molpai*, and their design was an integral part of the choreography. Their structure allowed architectural shapes to form when the dancers were static and provided weight and substance in movement.

The Ted Shawn Costume Collection houses three partial sets of these trousers made for different tours and casts performing this work. The first two sets are both high-waisted, flared trousers made from tan-colored cotton moleskin and are almost identical, except for slight differences in the weight and color of the fabric. Three pairs are made from a pale-tan moleskin and contain the initials of members of the first cast, from 1935. They are very worn and have multiple patches and repairs. Former Men Dancer Barton Mumaw recalled that the trousers were tightly fitted around the hip and thighs and that "a deep plié in second position would split that mid-section of the garment wide open."[1] The second set consists of four pairs made in the same pattern but in slightly darker and softer fabric. This set shows fewer signs of wear.

The third set are similar in shape and pattern to the first two but are made from a heavy brown, raw silk cloth and show limited wear. This softer fabric would have created a very different look than the earlier cotton moleskin version. The silk trousers were made from fabric woven by Eva Palmer Sikelianos (1874–1952), a prolific promoter of classical Greek culture. From the summer of 1939 until spring 1941, Sikelianos worked with Ted Shawn and wove hundreds of yards of fabric over that time. This fabric was used to make costumes for *Isaiah 52:1–7*, the chorus of *The Persians*, and *Kinetic Molpai*.[2]

1. Barton Mumaw, "Costume: Ruth St. Denis, Ted Shawn, Men Dancers," lecture notes, Spring 1984, 189.43, p. 2, Barton Mumaw Collection, Jacob's Pillow Dance Festival Archives.

2. Artemis Leontis, *Eva Palmer Sikelianos: A Life in Ruins* (Princeton, NJ: Princeton University Press, 2019), 185.

Olympiad, A Sports Suite, from O, Libertad!, 1936

COMPANY
Ted Shawn and His Men Dancers

CHOREOGRAPHER
Dennis Landers

COMPOSER
Jess Meeker

DESIGNER
George Horn

MAKER
Mansco, The Manhattan Shirt Co.

Shorts and sweater worn by Barton Mumaw and Frank Delmar in the "Basketball" section of *Olympiad, A Sports Suite*, performed as part of *O, Libertad!*, 1936

Cotton, wool, metal fastenings

Ted Shawn Costume Collection, Jacob's Pillow Dance Festival Archives, C-305_6-7, 306_5–6

Detail showing makeup stains on sweater worn by Barton Mumaw, C-305_6.

Shapiro Studios, Pittsfield, Massachusetts (American, c. 1929–1976), *Men Dancers in the "Basketball" Section of Olympiad*, 1936, photograph, $7\frac{7}{8} \times 9\frac{7}{8}$ in. (20 × 25.1 cm). Jacob's Pillow Dance Festival Archives.

The majority of the costumes for the Men Dancers were designed by Ted Shawn or by former dancer George Horn. Barton Mumaw, one of the Men Dancers, later recalled that Horn "had an outstanding ability to design and execute costumes and to devise everything from props to headdresses out of scraps."[1]

Due to their design and need for an exact fit, dance costumes often had to be custom made, but sometimes Horn was able to adapt items of ready-to-wear clothing. For the "Basketball" section of *Olympiad, A Sports Suite*, he appliquéd an orange felt letter *S* onto store-bought cream wool sweaters. The Ted Shawn Costume Collection also includes a second set of sweaters made from cotton and purchased from Vauxhall Sport Togs. It is unclear if these were worn for "Basketball" or for the "Cheerleader" section, in which the dancers wore similar sweaters but paired them with high-waisted cream corduroy trousers.

The basketball shorts were created from swim trunks made to order by Mansco, The Manhattan Shirt Co. Each pair contains the printed initials of the dancer for whom they were tailored. Despite being custom made, they were still altered later by Horn, who cut off and reset the waistbands to allow more movement, added darts, and applied orange stripes to each side.

1. Barton Mumaw and Jane Sherman, *Barton Mumaw, Dancer: From Denishawn to Jacob's Pillow and Beyond* (New York: Dance Horizons, 1986), 88.

S
S

The Jazz Decade, from O, Libertad!, 1936

COMPANY
Ted Shawn and His Men Dancers

CHOREOGRAPHER
Ted Shawn

COMPOSER
Jess Meeker

DESIGNER
George Horn

MASK MAKER
Mary Kinser

Jacket, breeches, and mask worn by Horace Jones, John Delmar, Wilbur McCormack, Frank Delmar, and Fred Hearn in *The Jazz Decade*, performed as part of *O, Libertad!*, 1936

Cotton, canvas, metal, elastic, and papier-mâché

Ted Shawn Costume Collection, Jacob's Pillow Dance Festival Archives. C-327_1-2, 328_1-2, 338_1-2

Detail from mask, C-328_2.

Shapiro Studios, Pittsfield, Massachusetts (American, c. 1929–1976), *Men Dancers in Jazz Decade from O, Libertad!*, 1937, photograph, 7⅞ x 10 in. (20 x 25.4 cm). Jacob's Pillow Dance Festival Archives.

***The Jazz Decade* was presented as part of Act II of the full-**length work *O, Libertad!* Program notes by Ted Shawn explained that "following the war comes The Jazz Decade in which eight masked figures give themselves to the cheap, shoddy, neurotic rhythms which were the aftermath of the war."[1]

The costumes, by former Men Dancer George Horn, were designed to echo these themes, giving the impression of cartoon figures in evening dress. Each dancer wore a short, tight-fitting white cotton jacket with long sleeves. The jacket resembles an evening shirt with bowtie and tuxedo jacket. The bottom of the jacket fastens to a pair of high-waisted black cotton breeches. There are six jackets and seven pairs of trousers in the Ted Shawn Costume Collection. In some cases, these items are labeled with two sets of names, showing how casting changed over time.

The most striking aspect of these costumes are the masks made by a childhood friend of Barton Mumaw's, Mary Kinser. They are decorated with highly stylized features, including downturned eyes with long lashes, angular eyebrows and noses, parted black hair, and three small red circles forming a mouth. The masks appear to be made of a shaped and hardened canvas and were designed to fit closely to the wearers head with no fastenings. The collection holds eleven of these masks, which appear to come from two different sets made for the work. They all show signs of wear and repair. The masks would have covered the ears and provided very limited sightlines—they would have been quite a challenge to dance in.

1. Ted Shawn, "Program Notes for O, Libertad," Berkshire Symphonic Festival, 1938, Springfield College Archives and Special Collections. For more on the racial undertones of Shawn's critique of jazz music and dance, see Ted Shawn, *The American Ballet* (New York: Henry Holt, 1926), 7–8, 22; and Robin Veder, *The Living Line: Modern Art and the Economy of Energy* (Hanover, NH: Dartmouth College Press, 2015), 255–56.

Contentious Histories

in Emergent Archives, a Dialogue

Munjulika R. Tarah, Erica Dankmeyer,
Thandi Steele, Panalee Maskati

The impulse to archive and to reenter and retrieve, and in some cases, the need or even moral imperative to do so, is fraught with practical, philosophical, and political problems, yet it remains compelling. It is further complicated by continuing definitions and reconfigurations of history, archive, and bodied cognition.

—Linda Caruso Haviland

This essay is based on a series of conversations that took place between November 2020 and January 2021. We began with broad discussions reflecting the critical issues in our encounters with the *Dance We Must* exhibition at the Williams College Museum of Art (WCMA), both in teaching with it (Munjulika R. Tarah and Erica Dankmeyer, in 2018) and engaging with the exhibition's archive (Thandi Steele '22, in 2020). Then we identified recurring pedagogical themes and core questions that emerged in our conversations and contextualized our inquiry within historical perspectives. We also invited Panalee Maskati '20, who researched and embodied this legacy as a student, to submit her reflections. In this exploratory, collaborative project as scholars, artists, and students of dance, we intentionally privileged our embodied and felt experiences—a perspective that is often missing from museum exhibitions, scholarly archives, and historical accounts.

Archival Ambivalence

MUNJULIKA R. TARAH When I initially walked into the *Dance We Must* exhibition, my first thought was that the materials and the history they embodied were so rich. I was grappling with the overwhelming amount of information present in the exhibit, and also had in my mind discourses about Ruth St. Denis and Ted Shawn in the context of colonial-era Orientalism, identity, and appropriation (fig. 4.1). I felt as if I could have taught a whole semester of classes on this one exhibition. It gave me the feeling of looking into two mirrors placed opposite each other and seeing infinite reflections, as if I was staring at something specific and also seeing many things behind it. St. Denis is a figure with whom I started my dance history journey, so I've engaged deeply with the sociohistorical issues related specifically to her work (and, to a lesser degree, Shawn's). In those first moments, as a South Asian person, I felt an interesting kind of unease experiencing these materials in this context. Opposite the gallery entrance was the Indian-inspired *Nautch Dance* costume (ca. 1920, see p. 24), installed with a large fabric background, accompanied by footage of St. Denis performing the *Nautch Dance* from 1944 (fig. 4.2). This installation was near the Chinese-inspired *Kuan-Yin* costume (c. 1919, see figs. 3.19–23), as well as life-size paintings of Shawn and St. Denis by Albert Herter (see figs. 3.1, 3.17). The elaborate displays appeared grand and a bit intimidating. Beyond this initial reaction, I was interested to understand the frameworks

FIG. 4.1, FACING
Franklin Price Knott (American, 1854–1930), *Ruth St. Denis and Ted Shawn*, 1916, color lithograph after an autochrome published in *National Geographic*, sheet: 10¼ × 7⅝ in. (26 × 19.4 cm). Jacob's Pillow Dance Festival Archives.

FIG. 4.2
Nautch Dance costume and props installed in the *Dance We Must* exhibition, Williams College Museum of Art, 2018.

and mechanisms through which specific meanings were going to be generated through the curation of the exhibition.

ERICA DANKMEYER As I moved among these costumes, photographs, films, and objects, the proprioceptive experience was both intimately familiar and surreal. The costumes, with their sweat stains, along with the images and films are all a record of an embodied, and not simply recorded, history. Representing realities and historical erasures in ways no written record can, these artifacts reperform St. Denis and Shawn but are also haunted by countless invisible personages. The opening of 36 trunks containing around 2,500 costume pieces from the Denishawn legacy feels, for some of us in the dance community, like a major archeological find akin to the discovery of Tutankhamun's tomb. Imagining the unpacking process conjured, for me, a performative moment when this material emerged, already in motion, anticipating its own revival. Ideas generated by these bodies, bodies that moved many to action, pushed modern dance to evolve as an art form. Yet multiple narratives are visible in your mirrors, Munjuli, reflecting some of the most complex and uncomfortable aspects of this history.

I begin to wonder: How would I conceive an exhibition of these materials that reflects the critical contributions of the Denishawn era while providing content about little-known contributors to its legacy and the conundrums of cultural appropriation? The lifelong commitment of both St. Denis and Shawn to dance as being critical to human life, was, given their historical moment and place, superhuman. Even today, dance is sometimes the ignored stepchild in the attic, while other art forms are met squarely in the front room. Advocating for the elevation of dance in society, and the very act of living a life dedicated to dance, required bold sacrifice. Yet these artists are among many choreographers who exploited the popularity of Orientalism among the elite, who felt entitled to their interpretations of cultural capital while dancing upon absent bodies and histories. How do we consider, and frame for others, the intention behind a dance work at the moment of its conception? These artists were products of, and fiscally reliant upon, the white privilege they inherited and capitalized upon.

THANDI STEELE Because I was not able to see *Dance We Must* in person, my perspective comes from the dance courses I have taken and my review of the exhibition via archival images. When I carefully observe each installation photograph from the archive, although I am briefly transported to the exhibition, I can't help but notice what is missing. So many questions are left unanswered. I yearn to ask St. Denis: Was there one particular costume you noticed that you knew you wanted to recreate, or were you inspired by a multitude of the beautiful pieces worn by the people you interacted with? Who helped you construct these garments and accessories? If we were to see a list of the names of everyone who helped you create your costumes, from the people who you saw clothed in similar pieces, to the people who helped you assemble them, whose names would we see on that list? Did you know their names? When you traveled on your tour through "the Orient" (fig. 4.3), how did you interact with the people native to the lands you were visiting? Did your languages align, or did you communicate through other means such as glances, facial expressions, or even dance? How did they feel about you, a white woman performing dances inspired by their own cultures, traditions, and histories? Were they disgusted, shocked, or surprised to see you performing dances like the nautch or *Radha* (see figs. 3.4, 4.8), or were they enthused to see a Western woman taking an interest in their culture? How did you feel when you laid your eyes on their bodies, clothes, and beings? I wonder: Did your world suddenly feel small?

FIG. 4.3
Photographer not identified, *Ruth St. Denis and Ted Shawn in Yangon, Myanmar*, 1926, photograph, $4\frac{1}{4} \times 3\frac{1}{8}$ in. (10.8 × 7.9 cm). Jacob's Pillow Dance Festival Archives.

These are the questions I wonder about the most, and yet they are mostly left unanswered in the archives we have access to today. My questions focus on those who helped St. Denis obtain her success, yet much of the literature surrounding her distances her from these unseen individuals in supporting roles.

DANKMEYER *Dance We Must* asks us to consider how we assign value, especially in a largely ephemeral art form. Linda Murray, curator of the Jerome Robbins Dance Division of the New York Public Library of the Performing

Interlude One

Panalee Maskati I was slightly baffled when I returned to the introduction to *Dance We Must* on the WCMA website. I'd been so sure that the exhibition had, at least in part, been framed as a "celebration" (fig. 4.4). Yet I found myself scanning a description washed of any implication of festivity. The museum's role is neutrally described as to "conserve, research and fully catalogue" the archival materials, and the stated intent of the exhibition—to "raise questions of imperialism, colonization, and racism"—is politically correct. It gives me pause for a moment, to find my most salient memory of the event, and what I think is the main source of my unease with it, absent from the official narrative of the exhibition. Of course, it has been three years. Perhaps that air of festivity I remember is a mirage, and the real substance of the exhibition was the version of events presented in the archives: an interrogation of the legacy and reality of imperialism that supports Western cultural institutions such as WCMA and Jacob's Pillow. If so, then perhaps the question to ask is: What is the role of entertainment and spectacle in reckoning with colonial history within the context of cultural institutions that are part of the architecture of Western empire?

FIG. 4.4
Panalee Maskati '20 performing a Ruth St. Denis solo at the opening of the *Dance We Must* exhibition, Williams College Museum of Art, July 2, 2018.

Arts, writes, "Archiving is an act of remembrance."[1] Giving the public access to these memories assumes the objects in the collection are worth something. They are certainly worth something to me, but many would not share my desire to consume this material. Its value, financial considerations aside, is a particular version of living history manifest, a curated presence within a suspended narrative. What does it mean for me to value art that represents harm and erasure?

St. Denis and Shawn were ahead of their time in terms of assigning monetary value to their (often appropriated) intellectual property. One of the ways they were able to survive as artists and maintain their school was to sell the rights to their dances. Any Denishawn dancer who wanted to teach the company's class content and structure, or to dance works from their repertoire, had to pay. *Dance We Must* presented, for example, a package of the instructional materials Denishawn sold for the 1922 piece *Maria-Mari* (fig. 4.5).

But in monetizing their work, St. Denis and Shawn also relinquished control over how that work would be taught and/or performed. The Jacob's Pillow Dance Festival Archives provided me with copies of the package for St. Denis's *Bakawali Nautch* (1913), which includes the musical score (within which additional unattributed handwritten notations appear), a text discussing the dance and its meaning (noting specifics such as the execution of "the beating of the

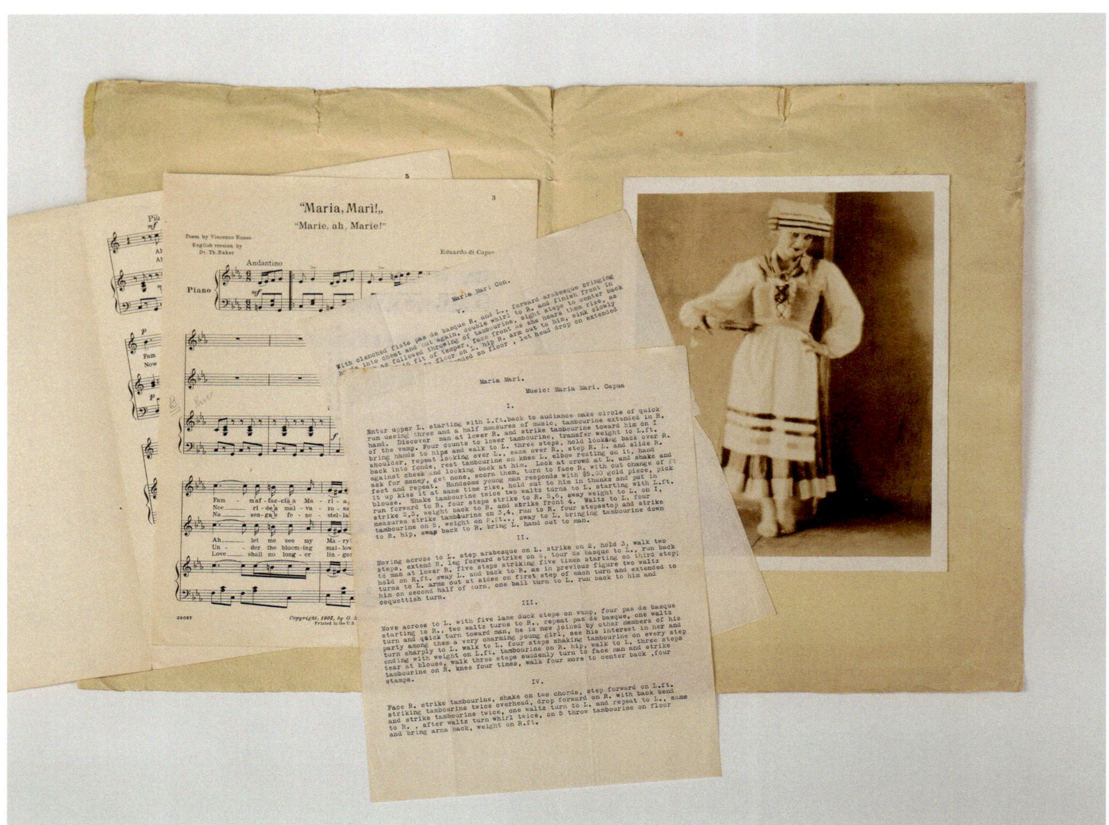

FIG. 4.5
Denishawn instructional materials for *Maria-Mari*. Jacob's Pillow Dance Festival Archives.

feet"), and a numbered, step-by-step description of the dance. Also included was a series of photographs of St. Denis, in costume, demonstrating positions from the dance. Today, bodies of repertoire being reperformed are protected by specific parameters, such as who is dancing, who is coaching, and prescriptive performance values (costume, lighting), in addition to licensing fees. I wonder what, exactly, did St. Denis and Shawn feel was "worth something" in the historical record? What material did they throw into the bonfire they famously built, marking the end of Denishawn and their partnership?[2] Could they have imagined our lasting interest, our obsessive connection to materials that can make history more real and tangible for us?

TARAH Those are interesting points of exploration, Erica! Because we are obsessively connected to these historical materials, and they are so valuable to us, often we feel these are not things we can question. The permission or encouragement to question was something I was thinking about a lot as I engaged with the exhibition and thought about what my/our pedagogical strategy would be. I believe my discomfort with *Dance We Must* was partly related to determining how I should present something like this to my students. There was so much background I felt students needed in order to understand the importance of an exhibition like this. At first, the exhibition felt kind of flat in comparison to the many years of history that scholars like Erica and I have studied. For example, the video of *Nautch Dance* that accompanied the *Nautch* costume has a complicated history within a colonial context. What was referred to as "nautch" by white people at that time was not a specific technique or dance form but an eclectic mix of movements embodied by lower-class, often lower-caste women dancers who primarily performed in the streets of India as a way to earn income. The instance of a white woman like St. Denis performing "nautch" in colonial India in the presence of an Indian audience, is to me a specific kind of parody that needs to be understood against many layers of racial and political hierarchy. These histories felt very present for me in *Dance We Must*, but they were not fully acknowledged in the exhibition's didactic materials or the presentation of the costumes and archival objects.

DANKMEYER These less-visible histories you mention, Munjuli, also seem to be depicted in divergent ways in terms of the exhibition's two gallery spaces. Compared to the vibrant blue gallery focused on St. Denis and Denishawn (fig. 4.6), the Men Dancers gallery felt calmer and more in scale with the people portrayed. I was struck by how tiny some of the men's costumes were. It seemed impossible that even a very slight male dancer could fit into them! That part of the exhibition also provided insight into a very human aspect of Shawn's legacy, his homoerotic artistic pursuits, as evident in photographs and subject matter (fig. 4.7). Here we had a window into the daily activities and artistic production at Jacob's Pillow, including footage of men dancing works created for them by Shawn. I'm fascinated by his ability to live his identity within the threat of a shaming society by creating the Pillow, a white utopian space, isolated not only from society but from the rest of dance and art making

FIG. 4.6
Installation view of the *Dance We Must* exhibition, Williams College Museum of Art, 2018.

FIG. 4.7
Earle Forbes (American, 1897–1970), *Nude Study of Barton Mumaw*, c. 1940, photograph, 10 × 8 in. (25.4 × 20.3 cm). Jacob's Pillow Dance Festival Archives.

in general. Here, (white) men could be dancers and lovers. They could, in the hills of the Berkshires, live, work, and perform for a select audience in ways that they could not in society.

Jennifer Edwards, in her essay "Culture in Context as Import, and in Exchange," points out that Shawn:

> (conveyed) a narrative that others have articulated as well—that dance somehow exists outside the confines of race, creed, and class. This perspective weaves a utopic view of dancers coming together, in spaces like the Pillow, and then transcending the structures of society. The idea is that the act of dancing levels the inequities of society itself. However, this is a notion that only people who enter every space with the freedom of white privilege can dream to be true.[3]

This dream, even for the white privileged, was more fantasy than reality. I wonder, were the summers at the Pillow a time out of time for the men? To what degree did this rarified space evaporate when they returned to the other parts of their lives? Even when they were touring Shawn's works, their behavior must have been altered within less safe surroundings. How did they navigate society in a professional pursuit not seen as "masculine," and how did they support themselves outside of dance?

STEELE When I think of Ruth St. Denis, I immediately think of the people with whom she worked and from whom she took her work, but this is complicated in a museum setting. Before examining the *Dance We Must* exhibition archives, I learned about St. Denis's and Shawn's legacy through dance courses at Williams College. However, if I had walked into that exhibition without this background information, I would have contextualized my view of the dancers based only on what was presented by the museum. Recognizing that many individuals might have had their first encounter with St. Denis and Shawn at this exhibition, the curators must have had to think deeply about the question: What do we want people's first interactions with this material to be? How do we want to portray St. Denis, Shawn, and what they stand for? I'm grateful for my previous exposure to these artists, because I feel if I had walked into the exhibition without background knowledge, I would have had a very different experience—one that would necessarily not have been nearly as critical, because I simply wouldn't have had enough contextual information to properly engage with it.

DANKMEYER Tensions around the reception of *Dance We Must* reveal the curatorial challenges posed by artworks implicated in complex histories of racist and colonialist cultural production. Despite the curators' acknowledgement of the problematic aspects of St. Denis's and Shawn's work, ultimately, many viewers felt the exhibition didn't go far enough in grappling with these histories. For example, many of the objects in the exhibition were placed on raised platforms, "on stage." This reverential approach, compounded by a lack of visual and written material providing cultural context for the inspiration for / sources of these objects and performances, prompted reactions of confusion and hurt on the part of some students, as expressed in an opinion piece written by Wilson Lam '21, a student intern at the museum at the time.[4]

TARAH In a fall 2020 class, we studied Melissa Blanco Borelli's book *She is Cuba*, about Cuban mulatta dancers, their history, and their role in Cuban society.[5] These dancers are most often presented as exoticized, and in talking about them to my class, Borelli used the term "enspectacularized," pointing to the process by which they were spectacularized repeatedly in performance and in historical archives. What Thandi said made me think of the decisions made by the curators and collaborators involved with *Dance We Must*. They made choices about which costumes would be presented and how they were to be organized in space, and those decisions visually "enspectacularized" St. Denis and Shawn again for a contemporary audience. St. Denis was spectacular as a performer, no doubt, but I think there was an opportunity in this exhibition to also say a bit more beyond the spectacular. For example, we might have learned more about St. Denis's other collaborators, as Thandi said earlier, or perhaps the role of Shawn and the Pillow in introducing dancers from different parts of the world to the US concert stage.

Centering the Peripheral

STEELE I have taken a class with each of you, Professor Munjuli and Professor Dankmeyer. In both courses we studied St. Denis and Denishawn, and although the classes were taught in very different manners, each of you did a phenomenal job of contextualizing their work. Professor Dankmeyer, we studied Ruth St. Denis at the beginning of our modern dance history course (Dance 205), and to this day whenever I think of St. Denis, I always think of Edna Guy, who offers an example of how St. Denis treated those who were not white. Guy was a talented Black American modern dance pioneer who turned to St. Denis, whom she idolized, for mentorship. Through a series of pen pal–like letters, St. Denis provided guidance to Guy. Yet when it came to actually mentoring or assisting with Guy's dance career, St. Denis disengaged, citing racial developments that needed to happen in order for Guy to succeed, and telling Guy she needed to grow up and see the world. For me, St. Denis's treatment of Guy resembles a white savior complex. St. Denis was more than willing to correspond through a few friendly letters. However, when it came time for taking action that could have given a young, Black, extremely talented dancer a shot, St. Denis became harsh and rigid, as if she were backpedaling on the confidence and promise she previously said she had seen in Guy.

Professor Munjuli, reading "Dancing Out the Difference: Cultural Imperialism and Ruth St. Denis's 'Radha'" by Jane Desmond was the beginning of my studies about St. Denis in your Asian/American Identities in Motion course (Dance 216).[6] After analyzing *Radha* through video footage and writing, the class's clear consensus was that St. Denis was appropriating a culture that was not her own and exoticizing a goddess of a religion she did not practice. We were interested in learning who had helped her create this work, because we knew it wasn't solely her invention. Looking back on the learning experiences cultivated in both your classes, I can detect the many decisions you made in order to provide the class with a solid understanding and contextualization of St. Denis, so we were not afraid to be critical and examine the entire picture.

TARAH It's really helpful to hear from you, Thandi, about what you remember from our classes, how we approached St. Denis, and this last point about the responsibilities and decisions related to pedagogy. For a teaching museum like WCMA, it's a tricky balance to try to cater to the larger Williamstown population and the Jacob's Pillow summer visitors, and also prioritize the students' pedagogy. Doing both can be difficult. In my experience, the exhibition felt like it was geared more toward the summer crowd.

Interlude Two

Maskati Pedestalized costumes, accessories, old documents, bright lights, larger-than-life video projections, hors d'oeuvres (was there food?), music, and the live performance that I was a part of were all technologies of spectacle designed to inspire awe and wonder—and to give people a good time. This intimacy between spectacle and critique, this performance of self-reflexivity that has become trendy among museums and other cultural organizations (*Dance We Must* isn't unusual in that way), feels specious to me. There are now market incentives and political pressure for museums to assume a critical attitude toward the colonial past, even to take on the role of cultural vanguard in revealing the "correct" takes on history to the general public, but are these gestures largely symbolic? How willing are museums to participate in the deconstruction and decentering of their cultural power and wealth?

DANKMEYER I love that you brought up Edna Guy, Thandi, and the record contained in the letters. In *Dance We Must*, some examples of that correspondence and images of Guy, for example, would have demonstrated the dissonance in this historical moment. As an idol to many, St. Denis galvanized and liberated the white women in her audiences, schools, and in the Denishawn company; company alumnae such as Martha Graham and Doris Humphrey went on to create their own progressive visions of art and womanhood. Yet the Guy letters implicate St. Denis in the prevailing racism of her time, perched as she was in her goddess role, safely avoiding what perhaps felt too complicated for her. Who would hold her accountable? Nonetheless, anyone who was defying the stereotype of the artist as degenerate—especially the dancer in the 1920s—contributed to progress, at least for some. All this gives us valuable insight into the current moment, in which arts organizations and academia are scrambling to reform unexamined racial and gender biases built into their foundations.

STEELE In addition to Edna Guy, we also know of a few others with whom St. Denis interacted in a similar power dynamic. In the book *Sweating Saris* by Priya Srinivasan, we learn the names of Mohammed Ismail, Mogul Khan, and Inayat Khan, three Indian men who accompanied St. Denis on her US tours between 1909 and 1914.[7] Srinivasan writes that Indian men had long been laboring in the United States, contributing to an increase in capital for white people for centuries. St. Denis took advantage of anti-Asian and anti-Indian sentiment in the United States as she used their racialized labor. She frequently performed with a group of "natives" who acted as part of her set in order to increase the perception of authenticity in her work (fig. 4.8). Many of these men were people she saw in New York and consulted for help with her performances and sets. They provided her with knowledge that allowed her to "assert her own authority in terms of economic and cultural capital,"[8] but did not receive any credit for their contributions to her success.

I want to name Mohammed Ismail, who questioned Ruth St. Denis's failure to acknowledge and compensate him monetarily. Remarkably, he decided to pursue legal action against her, even though there was no established legal precedent in terms of dance ownership at the time. An Indian man going into a courtroom against a white woman, especially during a time of extreme anti-Asian sentiments, had practically everything against him. In the end, he was not able to prove that he taught St. Denis any form of dance, and St. Denis continually asserted that she had learned what he claimed to have helped her with long before they met. Srinivasan observes:

> Only a white bourgeois woman such as St. Denis could be seen as a creator of "new" performance, because only such a person was viewed as capable of willfully constructing performances. Her labor was made visible while the Indian men's labor was simultaneously made invisible. St. Denis was thus the only body that could take on the role of a professional artist and seize power from "authentic"

FIG. 4.8
Photographer not identified, *Ruth St. Denis with Indian Actors in Radha*, 1904, photograph, 8 × 10 in. (21 × 26 cm). Jerome Robbins Dance Division, New York Public Library for the Performing Arts.

> male Indian bodies, who were ironically rendered "inauthentic" by profession.[9]

These men may have been some of the most valuable people to her in terms of her work and career, but she treated them as if they were valueless, benefiting from the widespread, racist American beliefs that upheld her position while simultaneously demeaning the men she worked with and took from.

TARAH That's a really relevant act of remembrance, Thandi, of naming Mohammad Ismail here in our conversation. I think it's important to acknowledge the elephant in the room: to me, the exhibition centered whiteness in its presentation. As we discussed, this was a museum project, not necessarily a dance studies or performance studies project where the body and its sociopolitical implications, for example in terms of race or gender, are prioritized. My interpretation of this object-related exhibition is that the costumes (not the raced bodies that filled the costumes) and the mythic personas of the two dancers were the focus. I do think there were avenues for engaging more with issues of race, appropriation, and colonialism, since there were already critical works in dance, performance, and cultural studies about St. Denis and Shawn that could have been consulted.

In *Sweating Saris*, Srinivasan also writes about "nautch" dancers from India who were brought to the United States in the early 1880s by impresario Augustin Daly, dancers who were described in the media as "exceedingly grotesque," "mulatto girls, who twisted their big ugly hands in the air with the grace of a cow."[10] She elaborates that these sentiments must be considered within the context of US Orientalism at that time, which was related to colonialism and anti-Asian sentiment; discrimination against Asians in immigration, citizenship, and naturalization laws of the twentieth century; and how dance reframed as labor fits into this history. This lens clarifies that the Indian "nautch" dancers' "work" in American theaters in the late nineteenth century had to be discredited or devalued in order to make space for the success of white dancers like St. Denis who built on, and obscured, their legacy.

STEELE As I analyze the *Dance We Must* exhibition, its racial and cultural connotations are directly correlated to my school of thought—one that actively resists the colonization of my own body and the bodies of other black and brown people around me. On the one hand, I recognize the greatness of St. Denis's feats. On the other, I understand that within a Eurocentric society, I cannot engage with her work without pondering critical questions that center the less-powerful individuals around her. Otherwise, I would not only be upholding the whitewashed ways in which we assign value to things, but additionally upholding them in my own mind. Every costume displayed in *Dance We Must* was a marvelous and intricately designed piece that felt like a small window into the world of the past, one I feel so distanced from but equally magnetized to by its beauty (fig. 4.9).

TARAH Thandi, the tension between beauty and critique you just mentioned might not be a tension actually, because as people who are trying to be historically informed, we have to examine why it is that we find something beautiful. What are the structures and mechanisms in our minds and in society that uphold *that* notion of beauty and not others? For example, the elaborate *Nautch Dance* costume in the exhibition, which on the surface is quite stunning, can be framed and curated so that the audience is primed to marvel. In that state of wonderment, the audience might miss the accompanying video of St. Denis performing the *Nautch Dance* where she embodies the gestures and expressions of Indian street dancers in a sort of discriminatory parody. To me, as a professor who was making it mandatory for the students in a dance history class to engage with the exhibition, it was imperative that I ask: How do I present something like this to our students within a complex historical and political framing so that they understand the underlying issues of colonialism, race, and inequality?

DANKMEYER Munjuli, your description of "discriminatory parody" in St. Denis's *Nautch* renderings reminds me of reactions I've had to watching her perform on film. She appears, to my biased eye, as flippant, even enervated, and seems unconcerned with her transitions between movements. Her personal charisma notwithstanding, and acknowledging the changes in dance technique over time, her approach does not appear, as we might say now, committed. She seems to try on a garment, temporarily assuming a role, rather than fully embodying it. And, of course, she cannot fully embody what is not

hers. Even St. Denis's posture often seems a bit hunched in a way that almost looks apologetic. All of this, and the bizarre moments when she's obviously talking to the camera, make it difficult for me to tell what, exactly, is going on in the records of her *Nautch Dance* performances.

FIG. 4.9
Installation view of the *Dance We Must* exhibition, Williams College Museum of Art, 2018.

TARAH Your confusion makes sense, Erica, because the word "nautch" is a colonial pronunciation of the word *naach*, which simply means dance in many South Asian languages. This term represents a colonial understanding of a wide variety of dances performed in public. The women dancers who performed under these circumstances were from marginalized classes and oppressed castes and were often considered unsophisticated, immoral, and "vulgar" by colonists and upper-class Indians. So, this idea of a nautch dancer being embodied by a white American woman is quite complicated within that historical context.

DANKMEYER *Dance We Must* featured archival materials from Denishawn's famed tour of India in 1925–26 (fig. 4.10). Among these were film clips of St. Denis, including a striking scene outdoors in Lahore, in which she is seated, on a chair, on the outside edge of a semicircle of musicians seated on the ground as they frame and accompany a dancer. The dancer mostly performs frontally, but occasionally turns in St. Denis's direction, as if acknowledging her as a privileged audience being given a special point of view. St. Denis is elevated visually because she has been given a chair, and

her pale ensemble contrasts with the darker colors worn by the performers. Yet, ironically, she also becomes part of the backdrop, the scenery, in the same way the Indian dancers she employed were used to perform mostly static background roles in dances such as *Delirium of the Senses*. At one point, particularly delighted with a specific gesture she has just observed, she gestures to someone off camera (a Denishawn dancer? Shawn?), making a quick demonstration with her hands, as if to say, "Let's keep that!"

FIG. 4.10
Photographer not identified, *Ruth St. Denis, Ted Shawn, and Denishawn Company Members Watch Dancers in India*, 1926, photograph, 5⅝ × 3½ in. (14.3 × 8.9 cm). Jacob's Pillow Dance Festival Archives.

STEELE I empathize with St. Denis's fascination with dances, fashion, and cultures that were vastly different from her own. I like to think that she was able to see a rich, captivating, and unique beauty that so much of the Western world throughout history (and today) understood as inferior, primitive, and unsophisticated. It is troubling to think about the losses people incur due to this backward mindset that often deems cultures with certain features less valuable.

DANKMEYER One of the most incredible parts of the exhibition for me was seeing the *Nautch Dance* costume juxtaposed with the archival footage of St. Denis performing *in the same costume*. The wall labels explained that she often decorated costumes with cheap dime-store finds, which she would transform into something opulent looking onstage. Conflicting feelings emerge. As a choreographer who has scraped costumes together with no budget, this resourcefulness resonated with me. Creating illusion is part of the art of the stage, and St. Denis gave audiences a live, animated view of fabrics and jewelry that fulfilled popular Orientalist aesthetics and fantasies. But what did re-creating the effect of an Indian nautch costume using such materials mean for St. Denis and her audience, and what does it mean today? Is Shawn's use of a colander to form a headpiece ingenious or depraved? These kinds of details make for rich classroom discussions about the complexity of art making, with considerations of authenticity, scarcity of financial support for the arts, the difference between homage and appropriation, and so on.

Interlude Three

Maskati As the vanishing points of so many histories, as the treasuries where the spoils of empire are hoarded still, museums are now taking on new forms of commemoration in a bid to maintain their moral legitimacy and epistemic authority amid language around power and oppression that is emerging in mainstream discourse. *Dance We Must* participated in this larger trend, a cultural paradigm that structures engagement with the history of colonization as a kind of visceral immersion in that history. It was a spectacular and powerful exhibition; in essence, the conversion of history into experience—sights and sounds, the tactility of the artifacts, all polished off with live performance. For such an experience to be cohesive and powerful, it must be scaffolded on a tidy narrative, one that lends moral legitimacy to the present by divorcing it from what is framed as a "finished" colonial history. This careful curation of the relationship between past and present provides an opening for institutions to lay claim to artists like Ruth St. Denis and Ted Shawn while distancing themselves from their more unsavory sides. It's a duplicitous move—the pretense of a century's progress—since the violence of the past, in fact, cuts deeply into our present. Does this exhibition ask what a material reckoning with this violence would constitute?

Colonial Contexts and Curriculum

TARAH Given my area of research and teaching, I felt hailed or "interpellated"[11] to engage with the exhibition, which gave me some anxiety, because I had just started in a tenure-track position at Williams College at that time! I felt like I couldn't not engage with it, so my strategy was to make sure that my/our students had substantial context before they walked into *Dance We Must*. In the history section of Foundations in Dance (Dance 100), for example, before we visited the exhibition, we read Brenda Dixon Gottschild's "Stripping the Emperor," where she discusses Africanist influences on ballet.[12] We talked about Orientalism and appropriation, with *La Bayadere* and Ballets Russes as a case study. We also read Jane Desmond's analysis of St. Denis's *Radha*, which discusses cultural imperialism,[13] and a section from Srinivasan's book *Sweating Saris*. We read from Susan Manning's *Modern Dance, Negro Dance*, where she talks about the influence of Black performers on modern dance.[14] To prime the students to think about the exhibition critically, we also had a set of questions they had to reflect on before they went into the exhibition. If I remember correctly, we had quite a rich and sometimes contentious discussion with our students and the exhibition curators. I thought the students were adequately informed and asked good questions.

FIG. 4.11
Installation view of the *Dance We Must* exhibition, Williams College Museum of Art, 2018.

STEELE Assigning the resources you mentioned above to your students provided important context, especially for those who may not have studied St. Denis's work previously. Reading and discussing such works gives individuals the power to think critically about what they are encountering, especially in a museum space that, historically, carries a degree of cultural authority.

DANKMEYER I was really grateful to collaborate with you, Munjuli, and our other dance colleagues to compose conversation points to contextualize the Foundations in Dance class visit to the exhibition. As the modern dance specialist in our department, I felt especially vulnerable. The students would have asked incisive questions, regardless of our guidance, because of the myriad influences on early modern dance we had discussed in class. But that course had to cover a broad spectrum of dance; as you noted early in this discussion, an entire course could have been created using this exhibition as a catalyst. The contentious and critical topics invited by the exhibition also have the potential to yield space for us to celebrate what was exceptional about these artists and their legacies. *Dance We Must* demonstrated how the future of modern dance encompassed both a rebellion against and an embrace of aspects of these aesthetics.

I never assume that people are educated about dance; even teaching at Williams, we find that our students have not had the opportunity to learn about its history and context. Sharing artifacts like those on view in *Dance We Must* (fig. 4.11), and exploring the multiple meanings therein, has the potential to inspire students to want to learn more about the influence and role of dance in society. The challenge is to simultaneously introduce unfamiliar modes of knowing while interrogating the material in ways that reveal its continuing relevance for viewers today.

The Feather of the Dawn

Just as Denishawn employed veils in its dances to create mystery and intrigue, the *Dance We Must* exhibition unveiled exquisitely restored and curated artifacts that nonetheless defied exposure, shrouded in multiple layers of meaning. To extract displaced and replicated histories from this unavoidably arbitrary grouping of objects, we cannot simply look. We must *feel*. And, therefore, while reanimating their veiled narratives, we cannot ignore that they have been inhabited by the bodies of dancers. Dance we must indeed, continuing a cycle of dialogues across time.

Notes

Epigraph: Linda Caruso Haviland, "Considering the Body as Archive," in *The Sentient Archive*, ed. Bill Bissell and Linda Caruso Haviland (Middletown, CT: Wesleyan University Press, 2018), 10.

1. Linda Murray, "Moving History: Dance and Remembrance," *Dance Index* 10 (Fall 2019): 5.

2. For more on the bonfire in which Shawn and St. Denis destroyed Denishawn materials upon the dissolution of their partnership, see Caroline Hamilton's essay in this volume, "'Fundamental Lines of Truth and Beauty': The Costumes of Ruth St. Denis, Denishawn, and Ted Shawn and His Men Dancers," pp. 35–45.

3. Jennifer Edwards, "Culture in Context as Import, and in Exchange," *Jacob's Pillow Dance Interactive* website, accessed February 10, 2020, http://danceinteractive.jacobspillow.org/themes-essays/dance-society/culture-in-context-as-import-and-in-exchange/.

4. Wilson Lam, "*Dance We Must* Struggles to Reconcile Art with Appropriation," *The Williams Record*, September 19, 2018, http://williamsrecord.com/230/arts/dance-we-must-struggles-to-reconcile-art-with-appropriation/.

5. Melissa Blanco Borelli, *She Is Cuba: A Genealogy of the Mulata Body* (London: Oxford University Press, 2016).

6. Jane Desmond, "Dancing Out the Difference: Cultural Imperialism and Ruth St. Denis's 'Radha' of 1906," *Signs: Journal of Women in Culture and Society* 17, no. 1 (1991): 28–49.

7. Priya Srinivasan, *Sweating Saris: Indian Dance as Transnational Labor* (Philadelphia: Temple University Press, 2011).

8. Srinivasan, *Sweating Saris*, 89.

9. Srinivasan, 91.

10. Srinivasan, 56.

11. Louis Althusser, "Ideology and Ideological State Apparatus (Notes Towards an Investigation)," in *Lenin and Philosophy and Other Essays* (New York: NYU Press, 2001), 85–126.

12. Brenda Dixon Gottschild, "Stripping the Emperor: The Africanist Presence in American Concert Dance," in *African Roots / American Cultures: Africa in the Creation of the Americas*, ed. Sheila S. Walker (Maryland: Rowman and Littlefield, 2001), 89–103.

13. Desmond, "Dancing Out the Difference."

14. Susan Manning, *Modern Dance, Negro Dance: Race in Motion* (Minneapolis: University of Minnesota Press, 2008).

Mary Harris Howry's Makeup Box

Makeup box owned by Denishawn dancer Mary Harris Howry (1892–1985), 1920s

Makeup box: imitation embossed red leather over cardboard core

Contents: pink tin canister containing Qui Sait Bath Powder (color: carnation), powder brush (possibly Japanese), sheepskin puff, pink velvet puff, bundle of black French pins, wrapped packet of Majesty black French pins, glass jar of Stein's Light Moist Rouge, two red and gold boxes of Powd'r Base by Hampden (one foundation and one rouge), packet of Kleenex Lipstick Tissues, silk stocking wig cap, red lacquer box containing black bobby pins and French pins, small red lacquer box of wooden sticks for mascara application

Inner box: medium-sized red lacquer box

Contents: small metal pot of Max Factor's Supreme Lining No. 6, metal pot of Premier 2 Lip Rouge prepared by the Lockwood Co., glass pot of Lashlux Black, metal pot of Inspiration by Richard Lloyd eye shadow in bronze, tube of Max Factor's Supreme Grease Paint No. 4½, small red lacquer box containing safety pins, brass Houbigant lipstick case

Ted Shawn Costume Collection, Jacob's Pillow Dance Festival Archives, C-577_1-23

Photographer not identified, *Denishawn Dancers: Anne Douglas, Jane Sherman, Geordie Graham, Ernestine Day, Edith James, and Pauline Lawrence*, 1926, photograph, 8 × 10 in. (20.3 × 25.4 cm). Jacob's Pillow Dance Festival Archives.

This makeup case and its contents belonged to Denishawn dancer Mary Harris Howry. Howry was hired for the 1925–26 East Asia tour and appears to have stayed with the company until 1927.[1]

These lacquered boxes were quite possibly bought by Howry on that first tour. The makeup in the boxes dates to the 1920s and includes various tubes of grease paint, solid sticks of foundation, powder, eye shadow, and lip rouge. Perhaps the most intriguing item is the glass pot of Lashux black and the small box of wooden sticks used to apply this to each eyelash. The box also contains hairpins and a wig cap as well as brushes and puffs.

Makeup for Ruth St. Denis, Ted Shawn, and their dancers was equally as important as costume. Howry's colleague Jane Sherman recalled that makeup was "Miss Ruth's special province. As new members joined the company for the first time, we were treated to a fascinating demonstration where the great lady of dance, wearing bathrobe and slippers, sat down before a mirror and dressing table covered with mysterious pots, pans, and powder puffs and showed us how she wanted us to look."[2]

1. Jane Sherman, *Soaring: The Diary and Letters of a Denishawn Dancer in the Far East, 1925–1926* (Middletown, CT: Wesleyan University Press, 1976), 9.

2. Jane Sherman, *The Drama of Denishawn Dance* (Middletown, CT: Wesleyan University Press, 1979), 12.

KLEENEX
Lipstick
MAJESTY
POWD'R • BASE

Contributors

Erica Dankmeyer is a former soloist with the Martha Graham Dance Company (1996–2006) and a regisseur of Graham repertoire. She is critically recognized for her reconstruction and performance of historic modern dance works. As an artist in residence at Williams College, her pedagogy includes modern dance technique, history, repertoire, and contemporary choreography.

Caroline Hamilton is a costume historian specializing in the design and construction of early twentieth-century ballet and modern dance costume. In 2018, she led the project to research, catalogue, and rehouse the extensive Jacob's Pillow costume collection. She is now the costume curator for the Jacob's Pillow Dance Festival Archives.

Panalee Maskati '20 majored in comparative literature at Williams College, where she was awarded the Hubbard Hutchinson Memorial Fellowship for excellence in dance studies and performance. Currently, she is involved in a research and performance project centered on disabled artists and performers in Bangkok, Thailand, and is also engaged in freelance translation.

Kevin M. Murphy is Eugénie Prendergast Senior Curator of American and European Art, Williams College Museum of Art. Prior to joining WCMA in 2013, he held curatorial positions at the Crystal Bridges Museum of American Art and the Huntington Library, Art Museum, and Botanical Gardens.

Norton Owen is a curator, writer, and archivist who has been associated with Jacob's Pillow since 1976. As director of preservation, he oversees projects involving documentation, exhibitions, audience engagement, and archival issues, as well as the extensive online archives and podcast series. He is the author of *A Certain Place: The Jacob's Pillow Story* and numerous other publications.

Thandi Steele '22 is a statistics and Chinese major at Williams College. Her dance studies include courses in dance ethnography and history, reflecting her continued interest in the role of dance in interdisciplinary inquiry.

Munjulika R. Tarah is assistant professor of dance history and theory at Williams College. Her research and pedagogy focuses on identity politics, nationhood, and dance in South Asia.

Image Credits

Unless otherwise noted, photographs of dance costumes, touring trunks, theatrical props, and of the *Dance We Must* exhibition are by Pivot Media and courtesy of Jacob's Pillow Dance Festival Archives. All images of artwork, historical photographs, and ephemeral material are courtesy of Jacob's Pillow Dance Festival Archives unless otherwise specified.

Figs. 2.2–5: Photo by Norton Owen
Figs. 3.1, 3.16, 3.17, 3.36, and 3.38: Courtesy of Williamstown Art Conservation Center
Figs. 3.4, 3.6, 3.20, 3.24, 3.26, 3.27, 3.30, 3.32, 3.34–37, 3.39, and 4.5, and page 123: Photo by David Dashiell
Fig. 3.5: © Musée Rodin. Photo by Jean de Calan
Fig. 3.7: © The Metropolitan Museum of Art. Image source: Art Resource, NY
Fig. 3.13: Photo by Petegorsky / Gipe
Fig. 3.31: © President and Fellows of Harvard College
Fig. 3.32: Courtesy of the Munson-Williams-Proctor Arts Institute / Art Resource, NY
Fig. 4.4: Photo by Bradley Wakoff
Page 21: Photo by Barbara Katus

Published following the exhibition *Dance We Must: Treasures from Jacob's Pillow, 1906–1940*, curated by Kevin M. Murphy and Caroline Hamilton, on view at the Williams College Museum of Art, June 29–November 11, 2018.

Generous support for this publication was provided by the Coby Foundation, Ltd.

Library of Congress Cataloging-in-Publication Data
Names: Murphy, Kevin M. (Kevin Michael), editor. | Hamilton, Caroline, 1988– editor. | Dankmeyer, Erica, author. | Maskati, Panalee, author. | Owen, Norton, author. | Steele, Thandi, author. | Tarah, Munjulika R., author.
Title: Dance we must : the art and costumes of Ruth St. Denis and Ted Shawn, 1906–1940 / edited by Kevin M. Murphy, Caroline Hamilton ; with contributions by Erica Dankmeyer, Panalee Maskati, Norton Owen, Thandi Steele, Munjulika R. Tarah.
Description: Williamstown, Massachusetts : Williams College Museum of Art, 2023. | Includes bibliographical references.
Identifiers: LCCN 2022017883 | ISBN 9781646570270 (hardcover)
Subjects: LCSH: St. Denis, Ruth, 1880–1968. | Shawn, Ted, 1891–1972. | Denishawn Dancers—History. | Ted Shawn and His Men Dancers—History. | Jacob's Pillow. Archives—Catalogs. | Jacob's Pillow Dance Festival—History. | Modern dance—United States—History. | Art and dance—United States—History. | Dance costume—United States—History. | Cultural appropriation—United States—History.
Classification: LCC GV1786.D43 D36 2023 | DDC 792.80973—dc23/eng/20220623
LC record available at https://lccn.loc.gov/2022017883

Published by Williams College Museum of Art
15 Lawrence Hall Drive, Suite 2
Williamstown, MA 01267
wcma.williams.edu

Distributed by ARTBOOK | D.A.P
75 Broad Street, Suite 630
New York, NY 10004
artbook.com

Produced by Lucia | Marquand, Seattle
luciamarquand.com

Edited by Kristin Swan
Designed by Ryan Polich
Typeset in Metro Nova by Maggie Lee
Proofread by Laura Lesswing
Color management by I/O Color, Seattle
Printed and bound in China by Artron Art Group

Cover: Details, Ted Shawn's *Cuadro Flamenco* costume, see pp. 46–51
Frontispiece: Front view, Ruth St. Denis's *O-Mika* costume, see pp. 28–33
Pages 4–5: Detail, fig. 2.1
Pages 10–11: Detail, fig. 3.20
Pages 12–13: Detail, Ted Shawn's *Cuadro Flamenco* costume, see pp. 46–51
Pages 34–35: Detail, Ted Shawn's *The Feather of the Dawn* costume, see pp. 52–55
Pages 58–59: Detail, Ruth St. Denis's *O-Mika* costume, see pp. 28–33
Pages 102–3: Detail, Ruth St. Denis's *Nautch Dance* costume, see pp. 24–27
Pages 124–25: Detail, fig. 2.6